Baseball, Battle, and a Bride
(An Okie in World War II)

by

James Bement

Order this book online at www.trafford.com
or email orders@trafford.com

Most Trafford titles are also available at major online book retailers.

Note for Librarians: A cataloguing record for this book is available from Library
and Archives Canada at www.collectionscanada.ca/amicus/index-e.html

Printed in Victoria, BC, Canada.

ISBN: 978-1-4269-2047-9

Library of Congress Control Number: 2009939011

*Our mission is to efficiently provide the world's finest, most comprehensive
book publishing service, enabling every author to experience success.
To find out how to publish your book, your way, and have it available
worldwide, visit us online at www.trafford.com*

Trafford rev. 10/21/2009

www.trafford.com

North America & international
toll-free: 1 888 232 4444 (USA & Canada)
phone: 250 383 6864 ♦ fax: 812 355 4082

To the Allied veterans of New Guinea, who fought in the most miserable of circumstances for little glory.

Contents

Preface

One Sunday in January 2009, fellow Draper Park Christian Church member Bob Freese and I were chatting after the service. I'd seen Bob and his wife Leona many times, and they were always pleasant and friendly. At the time, I couldn't have imagined what I was about to uncover from these two unassuming seniors. I noticed a red arrow emblem on the lapel of Bob's coat and inquired about it. That's when my education on Bob's experiences with the 32nd Infantry Division in the Pacific during World War II began. I stayed that morning, listening to his combat stories until everyone else had left the building. I told Bob that "*somebody*" should tell his story. As ministry leader of the church library and bookstore, retired military intelligence analyst, and student of history who's probably read hundreds of books on World War II, suddenly I realized that the "*somebody*" was me. With Bob being spry and mentally sharp, but not getting any younger at 92 years of age, I realized that despite everything else going on in my life, I had to clear my schedule and make room for Bob's story.

My initial thoughts were to interview Bob once or twice and determine if there was enough material for a book. If there was, my motivation would be to get the story of a member of "the greatest generation" told before it was lost, and tell the story of a real-life character, an unabashed "Okie" with a youthful sense of humor who somehow turned out all right in the end. Perhaps the story will be an inspiration to others. No matter what someone might be going through, no matter what they've done (even something like punching a superior officer and being court martialed), they might turn out just fine if they commit their ways to the One who created and loves them and stick with Him through the years.

As I interviewed Bob (often with Leona present), typically three hours a session in the mornings, when Bob was mentally the freshest, I realized much of what he had to tell would be of interest to others, but his stories had to be placed in context, nailed down with firm dates and locations. I'd need to conduct a lot of research in addition to the interviews. Unfortunately, a devastating fire at the National Personnel Records Center in St. Louis, Missouri, on July 12, 1973, destroyed millions of US military veterans' records, including 80% of the records from Army veterans who served between 1912 and 1960. No duplicate copies were made before the fire, not even microfilm copies. Therefore, like millions of other veterans, Bob Freese no longer has access to his service records. All he has is a few of his original service documents. The turning point in my research came when Bob and Leona found a bundle of letters from World War II, written from just a couple of months after Pearl Harbor, to Bob's discharge at the end of the war. Those letters helped immeasurably, by providing details both Bob and Leona had forgotten. In addition, I read every book I could get my hands on covering the New Guinea campaign and the 32nd Infantry Division, and spoke to Bob and Leona's daughter, Trish, and son, David, to gather stories they remember their dad telling, which Bob and Leona no longer remember themselves. Many times when I offered Bob a starting point from historical accounts, he'd be off and running, suddenly recalling another piece of the story.

After much deliberation and two aborted attempts to do otherwise, I made the decision to tell the story in the first person. The story flowed much better that way. Those who know Bob well may recognize that the language and grammar may not always be what Bob would've used, as Bob is a real honest-to-goodness, old-fashioned "Okie," with speech patterns to match. As Leona said recently of Bob, tongue-in-cheek, "A grammarian he ain't." Colorful, interesting, energetic, and clever, yes. Just not a "grammarian." While I hope we haven't lost too much of Bob's personality in the interest of readability, on the whole I believe the reader will appreciate the decision to go with the more readable alternative.

Obviously, others who were involved in the events described in the pages that follow will have their own memories. No two human beings view events in exactly the same way, especially after sixty-five or more years have passed since the events in question. The memories in this book are Robert and Leona Freese's alone, except for the historical accounts gained from other records. Even though I put the book together, writing in first person, it's based on many hours of interviews, and has been certified by Bob and Leona as an authentic account, to the best of their memories.

My hope and prayer is that this book will somehow bring honor and glory to Jesus the Christ (Bob and Leona's Savior and mine), recognition to an old veteran who served his country with distinction, and highlight the example of a lifetime of love Bob and Leona have shared together. They are interesting, colorful, and warm-hearted people. They are living history. I started out getting to know Bob and Leona primarily as historical subjects to interview, and as I spent more and more time with them, realized they are truly my friends.

James Bement
September 2009
Newalla, Oklahoma

Acknowledgments

I want to first thank Bob and Leona Freese for patiently enduring what no doubt seemed to them *endless* hours of interviews. They were always gracious, positive, and encouraging. Their enthusiasm for this project propelled me onward.

I gratefully acknowledge the kindness of volunteers who reviewed the manuscripts and provided useful comments and edits: Trish Carnes, Phil Crouch, Sherri Gambill, Merri Gambill, BJ Jackson, and Joyce Webb. Thanks to Matt Franklin for reviewing the primary baseball section (chapter 1), Janica Unruh for scanning in numerous personal photos provided by Bob and Leona, and Heath Bradford and BJ Jackson for cover ideas. Most helpful was Elizabeth Griffin, who reviewed the manuscript in detail twice, and provided many useful edits. Both times she worked against tight deadlines and beat them.

Many thanks to Terry Downard, my engineer friend from Tinker Air Force Base who allowed me to read (what was then) the entire draft to him on a six hour drive back from Whiteman Air Force Base, Missouri, one July day. That first marathon reading not only let me see how all the pieces fit together, but Terry offered important suggestions at a critical time in the development of the book.

Most of all I appreciate my loyal and patient wife Michelle, my lifelong mate, not only for her outstanding suggestions and edits to the manuscript, but for her understanding and love as I spent countless hours away from the family, immersed in this project.

From: Robert and Leona Freese
37 SE 37th Street
Oklahoma City, OK 73129

Subject: Authentication of the book *Baseball, Battle, and A Bride (An Okie in World War II)*

To: Trafford Publishing

We are happy to certify that the book written by James Bement entitled *Baseball, Battle, and a Bride (An Okie in World War II)* has our full endorsement, and is an authentic record as we remember the events described. We have cooperated with James throughout the process of compiling this book, and have provided letters written during World War II, photographs, mementos, and documents. In addition, we have participated in numerous interviews conducted by James, totaling approximately thirty hours, most of which, with our permission, James taped with an audio recorder.

We hereby certify that we have read a copy of the manuscript dated September 12th, 2009, and it is a true and accurate account of events, to the best of our memories.

Maurice Robert Freese

Maurice Robert Freese
Dated:
9-20-09

Leona R. Freese

Leona R. Freese
Dated: 9-26-09

Introduction

Almost every American has heard of the Marine Corps' battle for Guadalcanal, thanks to Hollywood and an excellent public relations campaign during World War II by the US Navy and Marine Corps. Fewer realize that while marines were fighting for that island, nine hundred miles away soldiers under General Douglas MacArthur were fighting a brutal campaign in New Guinea to keep the Japanese out of Australia and begin the Allies' slow roll-back of, until then, continuous Japanese advances.

Military historian Eric Bergerud called New Guinea, "some of the harshest terrain ever faced by land armies in the history of the war." Exhaustion and disease pushed American, Australian, and Japanese troops to the breaking point, even before combat began. Sixty-seven percent of the American troops who participated in the battles for Buna and Sanananda on the northeast coast of New Guinea contracted malaria.[1] Bob Freese was one of them. Though relatively few Americans know much about the Battle of Buna, casualties were considerably higher than at Guadalcanal. Sixty thousand Americans fought on Guadalcanal, and 1,592 were killed. Another 4,183 were wounded in ground combat. Forty thousand Australians and Americans took part in the battle for Buna in New Guinea. Of those, 3,095 were killed in action and another 5,451 were wounded.[2] There's a reason it's called "Bloody

Buna." Given those statistics, it was safer to be a marine on Guadalcanal than a soldier in New Guinea.

You'd think the War Department would've called on a crack infantry division highly skilled in jungle warfare to take on the Japanese in the first major land offensive in the Pacific. Surprisingly, it was the 32nd Infantry Division they pressed into service, a National Guard unit pitifully ill-equipped and untrained for that sort of warfare. One reason behind this may have been the January 1942 agreement between President Roosevelt and Prime Minister Churchill, to send the bulk of American support to the European Theater, and defeat the Nazis first. The Pacific theater of this World War would have to make do. In addition, the Army placed little emphasis on jungle warfare, and even less on training in the extreme conditions in which the 32nd Infantry Division found itself. The Allies had to figure it out as they went, and those lessons were painful. Bob Freese is proud to have been there, to have been part of the first major battle to turn the tide on the Japanese advance and change the course of World War II. This is his story.

CHAPTER ONE:
LIFE IN OKLAHOMA

It was the top of the 11th inning when I stepped up to the plate. Holt and Thompson were on third and second respectively, but we already had two outs. My team, the Oklahoma Natural Gas "Gassers," was tied 6-6 with the Bell Clothiers in an Oklahoma City Commercial League baseball game. The game had gone into the 11th when I snagged a high pop fly at first base to end the 10th inning. I was in my element here at Sandlot Park. The heft and balance of the bat in my hands felt just right. I was confident and strong. I loved the smell of the freshly cut grass, the cool evening breeze, and the excitement of the lights. I loved the rumble of the crowd. They were restless and eager, bantering, shouting, and calling out for or against the Gassers, the Clothiers, or individual players. Not a fan left the stands as the game came down to the wire. Above the rumble I heard someone call out encouragingly from the bleachers, "C'mon Robert, let's get a hit now. You can do it." I was relaxed and happy. It was Friday, the 13th of June 1947. I was putting my life back together after being discharged from the Army twenty-one months before. I had survived some of the most brutal combat in the Pacific. I had taken lives and had at one time written off any chance of making it back to Oklahoma. Now, I was in my own environment again.

Everything but the game flew from my mind as I turned to face the relief pitcher, Tom Kruta. Tom was well-known in the league, and I'd faced him many times. I knew him to be a friendly guy off the field, but on the mound he was my adversary. He looked intense, even threatening, as he focused all his energies on me, and my demise. His eyes bored into mine. He wanted me to strike out, to lose the game. I had no intention of fulfilling his wish. Kruta hurled a hard curveball that broke to the outside. Ball one. I kicked into the dirt with my left cleat, setting my right foot down into the back of the batter's box. The bat vibrated slightly a few inches from my right ear as I waited. Kruta reared back and blasted a fastball. I swung hard, and missed it completely. As Tom grinned, I thought, "Now THAT was fast. This guy really has an arm." The count was one and one.

Three pitches later it was three and two. Full count. Holt and Thompson led off third and second, ready to move as the next pitch was thrown. Bob Holt and Eddie Thompson were fast, and I knew they'd both stolen their share of bases this season. They'd try hard to score on anything I hit. Bob inched toward home, eagerly, anticipating what would happen next between Kruta an me. Suddenly, Tom Kruta wheeled right and fired to third as Holt dove headfirst, sliding back to third a fraction of a second before the ball snapped into the third baseman's mitt. Safe! I was relieved. It would've been disappointing to lose the game to a mistake like that. Bob had just led off third a bit too much. I stepped back to the plate, giving the bat a couple of half-swing chokes. I could feel hundreds of pairs of eyes on me. It didn't bother me— I loved the excitement. Holt and Thompson led off again. Tom held the ball tightly in his right hand, inside his left glove in front of him. He leaned slightly forward, briefly fixing a penetrating gaze at me, trying to un- nerve me, then he reared back and fired. A curveball. I was ready. Crack! As I nailed a solid line drive over Clothier shortstop Ken Pryor's head into left field, Holt and Thompson were already well on their way toward home. Bob Holt scored easily, and Thompson was right behind. The left fielder scooped up the ball, then ran forward to get some momentum and whipped the ball as far as he could, all the way to home plate. I rounded first as Thompson slid home in a cloud of red Oklahoma dust. Almost simultaneously the umpire yelled "SAFE!" and the catcher whirled to the right and side-armed the ball toward first. I knew I couldn't make second and was already hurrying back to first. I safely tapped the base with my left foot a half second before the ball arrived. I had driven in two runs, and it felt good. That turned out to be the game winner, as the Clothiers failed to get any action in the bottom of the 11th, and we won the game 8-6. [1] It was the Gassers' tenth straight win.

It seemed to me I was born with baseball in my blood. Even during the Depression I was so busy playing ball that I didn't pay much attention to all the things I didn't have. But then I suppose I was a little better off than most Depression-era young men, as I made some money playing baseball, getting paid for what I loved to do. Life was good, until Pearl Harbor changed everything.

I was born Maurice Robert Freese in Oklahoma City in 1916, the second of five children in the family. I had an older brother, two younger brothers, and a younger sister, with the kids spread out quite a bit in age. My youngest brother was fourteen years younger than me, and the sole sister sixteen years younger. I'm not really sure why, but the youngest brother was the family pet, maybe because he was young and a boy, or maybe because he had such a winning personality. In any case, he got a lot of attention. The family moved three times within Oklahoma City before I was eighteen, but on my last day of high school my folks settled down at 101 SE 38th Street in Oklahoma City. A girl named Leona Nievar lived next door, but she was nine years younger and, to be honest, I didn't pay much attention to her. Leona later said I never even looked at her.

The house we lived in prior to 101 SE 38th Street was just three or four blocks away on 36th street, so I really grew up in Capitol Hill, where I still live. Capitol Hill is now just a neighborhood, but at one time it was a separate city, before merging with Oklahoma City. When I was growing up, everything south of the Canadian River, which flows through Oklahoma City, was considered the blue collar part of town. Northwest Oklahoma City was considered upper class; African-Americans lived in northeast Oklahoma City.

Many white people rarely saw a black person. There were different restrooms and water fountains for whites and blacks. Oklahoma was segregated. The University of Oklahoma, for example, didn't have its first black student until after World War II. As strange as it sounds now, that's the way it was back then. I didn't think about it much back then, and I suppose most

Americans who were brought up in that era just accepted it. But now, I think it was wrong to segregate people like that.

Growing up, my life revolved around sports, family, and church; in that order. My parents were life-long Baptists, and my father was a head deacon, first at Capitol Hill Baptist Church and later at South Memorial Baptist Church. It seemed like we were always the first ones to arrive at the church and the last ones to leave. For years I was involved in church youth groups, and even there a lot revolved around sports. South Memorial Baptist Church had a baseball team, and I was one of their pitchers. I remember during one game I struck out eighteen batters, and yet the catcher was so bad that all eighteen got on base due to his errors. That was one of the worst games I was ever involved in.

In 1925, I put my trust in Jesus Christ as my Savior and was baptized. That was a significant day in my life, but for many years my faith was really not all that important to me. I went through the motions, like many kids do, but years later in New Guinea I would think much more about what God meant to me. My parents' faith would definitely become my own. But it would take the profound emotional experiences of a war where I was brought face-to-face with my own mortality to prompt me to a deeper level of spiritual maturity. As a youth I just sort of went with the flow. I was young, invincible. I suppose most kids think they are. I thought there'd be time later to think more carefully about spiritual things. Later, after my youth. After baseball. Many of my army buddies didn't enjoy the advantage of an upbringing in a Christian home, and died on the battlefied as young men who had never made peace with their Creator.

From the 4th grade through junior high, I played softball. In high school it was baseball. Baseball and softball were enormously popular in Oklahoma, as they were throughout the nation. It's still said that baseball is America's pastime, but back then it really was, and Oklahoma was one of the leaders, producing considerable interest in the game and such stars as Micky Mantle, Pepper Martin, Bobby Murcer, Dizzy Dean (who was born in Arkansas but grew up in Oklahoma), Willie Stargell, and Johnny Bench. Although I played football and basketball in junior high and high school, baseball was my favorite sport. For me, there wasn't anything like it.

*   *   *   *

ONE DARK, STORMY AFTERNOON, when I was about eight years old, I was walking the six to eight blocks home from school when it started to hail. By this age I was well aware of the destruction Oklahoma hail can wreak, so I ran across the street and threw myself under a car parked alongside the curb. However, as soon as I got settled, to my horror, I heard the driver's side door open and then close above me. The engine quickly started, and the car began to move. I was frozen in terror. The car drove off down the street, leaving me lying on my stomach in the road. I don't think the driver ever saw me. I'm sure he would've been surprised had he looked in the rear view mirror and seen a small boy lying in the road where his car had been. Thankfully, back in those days cars were higher off the ground, and it missed me completely. It gave me quite a scare though, and after that, as I grew up, I was always very cautious when getting under a car to work on it. I always placed a block or brick behind each wheel. I had no desire to go through that again.

Still, a year or two later, walking home from Lee Elementary School, I ran across the road without paying attention to traffic and got hit by a car. This time I wouldn't escape so easily. The car seemed to come out of nowhere. I saw a red blur out of the left corner of my eye and almost simultaneously heard the screeching of brakes and felt a terrific impact, and then went tumbling down the road. A minute later as I laid in the middle of the road, I was dimly aware that quite a crowd was gathering. I slowly became aware of a white-haired old man with wire-rimmed glasses, who I took to be the driver, bending over me and repeating, "Are you alright son? I'm so sorry. I didn't see you." I don't remember how I got home, but I was in bed for four days with a bruised hip, bruised ribs, and a bruised ego. Of course, doctors were expensive, and most people just didn't go to the doctor back then unless it was absolutely necessary. At three dollars, an office visit seemed like a lot of money. In most cases if someone had, say, a broken leg, unless it was really bad they just let it mend on its own, and hoped for the best. If they ended up with a limp, that was just the way things were. And that was before America's Great Depression. For a lot of families, health care was almost a luxury. We'd never heard of medical insurance.

I was grateful that I wasn't seriously hurt, but right after being hit by the car I contracted the mumps and missed more school. The result was that I was held back half a grade. Today, most children begin a school grade together, in the Fall, and finish the school year in May or June. Back then you had two options, to start in the Fall or the Spring semester, and finish in June or December. So it put me back half a year. I had to sit through half of the fifth grade again, and didn't finish in May, but in December.

Of course, Oklahoma was and is known for its oil industry, and there were quite a few oil wells on the east side of town. Even during the Depression, despite the John Steinbeck image of Oklahoma as a backwards, desperate state, Oklahoma's oil industry actually grew. In 1930, Oklahoma City had about 800 oil derricks, harvesting the world's second-largest oilfield. By 1940, the number rose to 1,500 wells.[2] If workers left their gloves around a site, we kids would climb up the oil derricks and use the gloves to slide down the cables supporting the derricks. Back then, you could practically jump from one rig to the next. They were all over town, right in the middle of the city. British-American owned quite a few derricks in our neighborhood. When we lived on SE 38th street, there was a well no more than fifty feet across the street from our house, and another well right behind our house. Three pipelines ran along the edge of our property, one each for oil, salt water, and fresh water. All three were necessary for the well.

I remember one incident in March 1930, when I was thirteen years old, with a nearby well named "Wild Mary Sudik." One of the consequences of Oklahoma City sitting on one of the country's most productive oil fields is that wells sometimes went out of control. The exhausted crew of this southeast Oklahoma City well had already been on duty for twelve hours as they worked to remove the drill pipe and replace it with a permanent pipe on the more than 6,400-foot-deep well. Suddenly, gas under tremendous pressure rushed up from below and blew pipe and then oil and gas high into the sky. The plume, or gusher, shot up hundreds of feet and was visible for miles. It coated houses, cars, roads, and backyards with oil for miles around, though the winds must have been favorable for us, since it didn't "oil" our house. It ran wild for eleven days before it was capped, leaving huge pools of black, sticky oil. The well was on the Sudik farm, just a few miles east of our house, and of course it was big news. We had seen other gushers, but none that compared with the Wild Mary Sudik. Film of the gusher appeared in newsreels shown at theaters around the country. On the positive side, once "Wild Mary" was tamed, it became the most productive oil and gas well in the world. [3]

Leona's dad worked in the oil fields before the Depression. For a short time the family lived in the boom town of Seminole, sixty miles southeast of Oklahoma City. In 1926, Seminole grew from 800 to 10,000 people almost overnight; so fast that there weren't enough homes for the laborers. The fortunate ones lived in temporary houses called shotgun houses. That simply meant if you fired a shotgun through the front door, the pellets would fly right out the back door. It was just a few rooms in a row with no hallway. I suppose they were the forerunners to mobile homes. Leona's family wasn't fortunate enough to find a shotgun house in Seminole, so they lived in a big tent, about fifteen by twenty feet, with partitions for a bedroom and a kitchen. There were eight family members in that tent. It was part of a tent city, with similar tents "next door" to the Nievar family's tent, and hundreds of them altogether. Oil industry jobs were in high demand.

Drillers or rig builders could make $300 a month. Leona's father was a pumper, so when he worked in the oil business he earned $100 a month. That meant he drove from well to well checking and maintaining pumpjacks, motors, compressors, meters, dehydration units (systems that remove water from natural gas), and kept lines free from ice blockages, and so forth. It was much safer than being a driller or rig builder, and better for a family man, because he worked with established oil wells. I knew drillers who had to pack up and move the whole family if a job was out of town. In addition, being a pumper meant steady work, while many oil industry jobs were intermittent, due to the nature of drilling.

Later, during the Depression, Leona's father couldn't find work at all near Oklahoma City, so he followed the harvest, working on farms all the way up through Oklahoma, Kansas, and Nebraska. One time he was paid with a 100-pound sack of potatoes. For some reason, instead of converting it to cash, he brought it to the local rail station and had it shipped to Oklahoma City. Back then, 36th Street (Grand Boulevard) was the railroad's delivery limit, so Leona's mother told the railroad she'd have her boys take a wagon two blocks to 36th and Santa Fe and meet the delivery driver. However, they said for two blocks they'd make an exception, and the railroad delivered the "paycheck" right to the house. Leona used to say her family had beans and potatoes one day and potatoes and beans the next. Perhaps surprisingly, Leona still likes potatoes, but she "likes 'em seasoned up." Back then we used a little vinegar on white or brown beans as a cheap way to add some taste. Having some meat, like bacon, to go with the beans was a rare treat.

There wasn't always a lot of food in the Depression, but we never went hungry. I don't remember much about what we ate, but I do remember we had a nanny goat, because my sister needed goat's milk for some medical reason. We also had an old billy goat my brothers and I sold to the Oklahoma City Chief of Police, who lived a few blocks away. He wanted it for his son, as the goat pulled a two-wheeled cart, in which he thought his son would have fun riding. However, the goat was ornery, and within a week or two the Police Chief returned him. The Chief didn't even want his money back; he just asked us to take the billy goat off his hands. One time my family was out of town for a few days, while a neighbor across the street fed and watered the billy goat for us. We arrived home to find the old goat standing on the roof of our barn. I have no idea how he got up there.

The Depression was tough on Oklahoma, and those who didn't have much in the 1920's were even worse off in the 1930's. For many there just wasn't any work, and some were forced out of their homes. I remember there being what were called "Community Camps," "Hoovervilles," or "Ramshackle Camps" on the Canadian River just a few miles north of our home. People who had nowhere else to go built little shacks, maybe six by eight or eight by ten feet. They'd use any material they could scrounge: pieces of metal, wood, or anything else on hand. I don't remember any kids coming to school without shoes, and I don't remember ever being without shoes myself. It was in the Army that I needed shoes, but more on that later. Leona had to wear her older brother's hand-me-down, lace-up boots during the winter, and I suppose there were a lot of kids who weren't in the latest fashion. But that <u>was</u> the style back then. We made do.

During the Depression my Dad worked pretty steadily in the glass business, installing glass in houses and businesses. Sometimes I worked with him, and I also worked at two different grocery stores when I was young, but during my high school years and even afterward, baseball was my life. I played for many different teams, high school as well as city teams. During high school I played for my school, Capitol Hill, but I also played for Central High during the summers, as high school baseball continued on after school was let out for the summer. Also during the summers, I was in the Ban Johnson 19-and-Under League. I played for various Oklahoma City area teams, as well as small towns like Ardmore, Elk City, Enid, and Weatherford. Even small towns had good ball fields, and fans would pay to watch the games.

Baseball was big entertainment during the Depression. There were a number of large ball parks, many that held over a thousand fans. I remember an All-Star softball game at Wheeler Park in Oklahoma City, where the Oklahoma All-Stars played the Arizona All-Stars, and there were about 10,000 fans. The Oklahoma team managed only three hits, and lost the game 2-1. It was a bittersweet day for me, because I got two of the three hits, including a home run.

In baseball we normally played teams from Oklahoma, Texas, Kansas, and Missouri. I played a variety of positions, including pitcher, first base, and outfield. Although we often played in or against semi-pro teams, most of us were technically amatuers. I often played alongside men who were getting paid as semi-pros, but it was better to be an amatuer, because we could play in a lot more tournaments, and that's where the money really was.

Twenty year old Bob Freese (center top) with some teammates
from the Municipal Garage Baseball Club – 1937.

Some of us made fairly decent money playing "amatuer" ball. After a game, fans would give the coach money to distribute among team members, or to a particular player who'd done well. I think they were mainly grateful gamblers who had bet on the outcome of the game. I could get ten or fifteen dollars for a home run, and during one particularly exciting game against the Chicago Hottentots at Byerly Park, by the state capitol, I hit a home run in the 14th inning to win the game. I received the enormous sum of twenty dollars, almost as much in a few hours as my father made in a week. That was a lot of money back then. But of course baseball season was only May, June, and July, followed by tournament play. I loved the game and thought that getting paid for something I had so much fun doing was great. I played as much as I could, picking the teams that would offer me the best chances of making some cash. The various teams were in competition for the best players, so they tried to pay them what they could. Most of it was arranged beforehand. A team would tell me what position they needed, and sometimes even how much it would pay. The smaller teams like Weatherford, Enid, and Ardmore were often the best payers, probably so they could entice some of the better players to make the drive from Oklahoma City. Then, if you did well, you'd get a bonus. I suppose baseball as entertainment during the Depression was even more important in those small towns than it was in the city.

Normally, I had a pretty full schedule. Many Saturdays I played games for two or more different teams. I remember one Saturday, I played a double-header in Norman, just south of Oklahoma City, for one team, then drove over 100 miles north of Oklahoma City to Ponca City and played another double-header for another team. Later, one of the teams, the Gassers, tried everything under the sun to prove I played pro ball, to disqualify me. Oddly, this was one of the teams I played for after the war. When I played for Greenleaf Chevrolet, I always had a new car to drive, and twice I got good deals on almost new cars. Thanks to my baseball income, I was able to buy my parents a 1936 four-door sedan that the Greenleaf Chevrolet owner's wife had been driving, and later bought myself a gray 1937 two-door Chevrolet coupe which was about six months old. My baseball "career" also contributed to the family income, and given the difficult economic times, that made me feel pretty good.

Throughout the 1930s agricultural disaster ravaged northwestern Oklahoma, eastern Colorado, western Kansas, the Texas panhandle, and northeastern New Mexico. Extreme farming methods combined with record droughts to form a tragic episode in American history called the Dust Bowl. Although Oklahoma City was about 150 miles from the southeast edge of the Dust Bowl phenomenon, the walls of dust and dirt that swept through the area were so vast that they could turn day into night throughout the state. During one game in 1934, the Capitol Hill High School baseball team was playing Anadarko High School in Anadarko, about sixty miles southwest of our school. I was playing center field when a huge dark cloud approached. The area became so dark with dust and dirt that the infielders had to turn around and yell to the outfielders when someone hit the ball toward them. In most cases I didn't see the balls until they had gone past me. With visibility a matter of feet, there were a lot of home runs that game. When there was a cloud of dirt and dust rolling in, people would say "Here comes Kansas," or "Here comes Texas," depending on from which direction the dirt cloud was coming.

Being on the baseball team in high school was beneficial in many ways. In 11th and 12th grade I received special privileges, in particular from an English teacher named Mrs. Kinkade, who helped me make it through academically. Mrs. Kinkade was around so long that my daughter had her for English a generation later. She was known as a tough teacher, notorious for calling the sharpest students in the school "babies" who were spoiled and coddled, and she required a score of 97% to get an A. Some thought she harrased students in any way she could. But she liked me, so I got out of assignments, was excused to leave early for practice or games, and always made good grades in her class. Without her favors, I never would've passed English. I'd like to think it was my winning personality that won her over, but in reality, she gave the ball players special attention. Leona said football and baseball players habitually asked her to do their homework, so when she completed hers, she'd make an extra copy for the athlete. All he had to do was write his name on the top of the paper. In some classes it was institutionalized, in others it wasn't. More than one teacher expected the girls to share their homework with the ball players. Sports were very big back then. High school baseball games drew large crowds, even though there was a ten cent charge to attend tournament games. My brothers often came to my games, and my mother came to a number of daytime games, but I don't remember my dad being there very often. Every boy wants his dad to watch him play, but I understood my father was weighed down with the responsibility of feeding a family during the Depression.

I was having so much fun playing high school baseball my senior year that I came up with a plan to play an extra season. I was due to graduate in

December 1934. Though I was making an A in trigonometry, a class I needed, I dropped the class during the middle of the semester and failed to graduate with my peers. I ended up playing baseball another season, and earned my diploma in May 1935; I was almost nineteen by that time. I hate to admit it, but academics just weren't that important to me. Since I had no plans to attend college, being able to play an extra season on the high school team was worth putting up with school for another six months. I had a lot of fun.

After I graduated from Capitol Hill High in 1935, I lived with my parents and worked part-time for my dad while I played ball. My dad was a foreman at ACME glass and whenever he needed extra help cutting large quantities of glass in the shop he'd hire me. They'd get large shipments of glass in, and I'd cut it by hand with a glass cutter to the various sizes needed.

Two years after high school, in 1937, an eighteen-year old scout for the Oklahoma Indians named Curt Gowdy saw me play baseball and gave me a chance to try out for the team. The Indians were an AA farm team for the Red Sox and others. The Indians played in the Texas League, and the year I graduated from high school they won the league championship. Curt Gowdy drove me to the Indians' spring training camp in Jacksonville, Texas, southeast of Dallas. On the trip down, to my surprise, he asked me to try out for catcher, and issued me a brand new catcher's mitt. Since I normally didn't play catcher and baseball gloves weren't always used before this time, breaking in the glove was a lot of work. When I first started breaking it in, the leather was so stiff the ball would bounce almost back to the pitcher. While by this time it was becoming common to see catchers and first basemen using gloves, it wasn't until a couple of years later that all players used them. Since I'd been playing for many years without a glove, most of my fingers had either been jammed or broken.

I was at the Jacksonville training camp for three or four weeks, staying in a hotel the team arranged for the players—the whole team was in the same hotel. We didn't stay there in Jacksonville the whole time though. We played exhibition games around Texas. The coach had me play in 90% of the games. I thought I played pretty well (once the stiff new glove was worked in), but I didn't make the team. The problem was that the Indians already had three catchers, and all three had played in the major leagues. I've always wondered why they asked me to try out for catcher when they already had three of them and it wasn't my normal position. I knew I had more of a chance making the team as an outfielder or first baseman, and if it had been another position, I believe I would have.

One result of my time in Texas was that St. Louis Cardinals third baseman Pepper Martin observed my performance and offered me a position on a Cardinals' farm team in Florida. Pepper Martin was quite a famous baseball player from Oklahoma who played in the 1928, 1931, and 1934 World Series, and was an All Star in 1933, 1934, 1935, and 1937. The pay on the farm team would've been just $50 a month (though almost twice what a US Army private earned, as I'd later find out), and I turned him down. I could make more money playing in the amateur league in Oklahoma, so I returned home. Years later, we heard Curt Gowdy on the radio, and later on TV. He turned out to be one of the most famous sports announcers in the US, and as he became well known I thought, "Hey, I know that guy." I understand he made it to the broadcasters' wing of the Baseball Hall of Fame.

Two quick final stories about baseball in those days. Around 1940, Leona's Uncle Burt married a lady named Mary, who Leona then knew as Aunt Mary, and only later did we find out Aunt Mary had been one of my biggest fans in the 1930s. She said if anyone ever disparaged Bob Freese, she'd get right in their face. Small world. Later, after our daughter Trish was born in 1946, a nurse helped Leona with a procedure in the hospital, and later Leona saw her at a ball game. The nurse said something to Leona about such and such player Bob Freese (I suppose I had a number on my uniform), and Leona asked, "How do you know my husband?" "Oh," the nurse said, "I always go to the games when he's playing." She had tracked my progress for years. That was a real honor.

*   *   *   *

My mother had cancer, so in 1940 my folks hired Leona, the next door neighbor, to do the ironing after school. She came over every Tuesday to work about an hour and a half for fifty cents. Now I saw her more often, but I still didn't pay much attention to her, except for teasing her. I remember once tying her shoe laces in a knot and then pouring a glass of water I had nearby on them to make them harder to untie. Leona acted upset and flustered, but I think she liked the attention. What she didn't like was our little family dog, Max. I don't think Max actually bit anyone in his life, but he was protective of me and often acted like he wanted to bite Leona. Leona called

Max a little smart-aleck mutt, and later claimed he was trying to warn her away from getting mixed up with me.

Although I gave Leona a ride to her high school choir events a few times, we only had one real date before the war. Since she was sixteen and I was twenty-five, it is remarkable that we even had the one. Leona told her "Mama," as Leona called her, that I'd asked her out, but her mom said, "Leona, he's not going to take you out. He's got other girls." But when I came to the door it happened so fast that Leona left the house before her mother could say no. I suppose Leona's mom would've said no in advance if she thought I would really show up, because I was an older man. We went to Hans Barbeque for dinner and then to a movie at the Criterion Theater. I had Leona back by midnight, and her mother never said a word about it. That was in October 1941, just three months before I was drafted.

CHAPTER TWO:
WORLD WAR II BEGINS

I was twenty-five when Pearl Harbor was attacked and the United States entered World War II. Though I was able bodied and single, and expected to be drafted, it happened much faster than I thought it would. I wasn't too happy about it. I was pretty independent at this point in my life and I had no ambition whatsoever to be told what to do by a bunch of sergeants. I hated being bossed around. Later in the Army I had trouble with officers because they expected me to salute them, and I didn't go for all that. All the saluting, yelling, inspections, calling to attention, nonsensical lectures, and so forth, sort of went against my grain. It's not that I wasn't patriotic. It's just that my independence meant a lot to me. Another thing I didn't like was that I went off to basic training alone. I didn't know a soul.

Our postman delivered the draft notice on the 8th of January 1942, just a month after the Pearl Harbor attack. I was instructed to report the very next day, January 9th. If the mail had been late, I would've been late to report. I drove my car down to the processing station on 6th and North Robinson in downtown Oklahoma City, and reported as instructed. I sat around most of the day, then had a medical exam. There wasn't much to it. There were no classification tests, no intelligence tests, no dexterity tests, no eye exams, no written tests of any kind. It was pretty basic. There was no question of passing or not passing. As I said later, "They told you to bend over, and you passed. You was in when you walked in." In the middle of the afternoon they said, "Go home and report tomorrow. You'll be shipped out to Fort Sill with some others." I drove home forlornly and parked my Chevrolet coupe in front of my parents' house. As I stepped out of the car, I knew it would probably be a long time before I had the freedom to drive it again. You take simple things like that for granted as a civilian. I walked in and handed my dad the keys. We didn't discuss him driving my car. I guess it was just assumed he would, and he drove it throughout my absence. My two-door coupe got better gas mileage than the larger family car, and gas was rationed during the war, so he drove the coupe to work every day. When I returned home from the war I had to replace the clutch, because my dad rode the clutch. I appreciated him taking care of it for me while I was gone though. There was no time to say goodbye to anyone else; my immediate family members were the only ones who knew I was leaving. I wasn't much for sad good-byes anyway. The family ate dinner together, then I went to bed. I had no time to mourn my freedom coming to an end.

On the 10th of January I rode a city bus to the military processing station downtown and reported at 0900. My father would've given me a ride, but he'd already left for work. I stepped onto the bus with no suitcase or luggage of any kind. All I had with me were the clothes on my back. Upon arrival, I found the military processing station was packed with men. After standing in a few lines, getting my blood type taken, and processing some paperwork, I was ordered to board a bus with about fifty other recruits. Soon we set out for Fort Sill in Lawton, Oklahoma.

The few days at Fort Sill were spent standing in lines to be issued various clothing articles and toiletries. I was given size 11 shoes, though I wore size 7 ½. They were so oversized I could do an about-face while my shoes stayed in place. I was stuck with those size 11s until I arrived in Australia four months later. Besides uniform issue, there were classic Army "buzz job" haircuts. Four or five barber chairs sat in a row, and one after the other, civilians came in as individuals, and filed out the other side of the room as nearly identical-looking basic trainees. I thought the barbers had the easiest jobs in the world. As recruits sat down, one after the other, a barber placed his left hand on his subject's head to steady it, with his right wielding the electric clippers. With a few quick half-circle strokes, he eliminated almost all the hair on a recruit's head. Zzzzst, Zzzzst, Zzzzst. It didn't matter if the man had a little hair or a lot. The haircut took the same amount of time. Since I kept my hair short and was getting a bit thin on top anyway, I wasn't concerned about the short haircut. Good thing, as there wasn't much left anyway. That night in the barracks, I observed how oddly-shaped some heads were without hair. Not only were there irregularities, but quite a few heads bore scars their owners were probably previously unaware they had. You realize how much a hairstyle can personalize someone's appearance when that option is gone. We got the message. We were no longer individuals.

The only other thing gained from Fort Sill was that we learned to form up in platoons and carry out some simple marching steps. I remember one poor farm boy who just couldn't seem to learn to stay in step. The drill sergeant called out, "Left, right, left, right," or, "One, two, three, four," and once most of us got that, just resorted to, "Hup, hoop, hreep, hoor," but the recruit didn't seem to know his left from his right foot. Most of us caught on quickly, as it was really pretty simple. Of course we were also motivated by the drill sergeant yelling and screaming profanities at any man who failed to catch on, with the drill sergeant's face about an inch from the offending trainee's. We quickly learned not to stand out. When the drill sergeant called "left," "one," or "hup," you were supposed to step forward with your left foot, then step forward with the right when he called "right" or "two," which came out like "hoop." "Hup, hoop, hreep, hoor...hup, hoop, hreep, hoor." Odd numbers meant left foot forward, even numbers meant right. More complex steps like "To the Rear, harch," were just too complicated for most of the men in that early stage of training and would be left for later. Except for the simple things described, the Army pretty much kept us trainees in the dark about their plans for us. All I knew was that I was now in the Army, property of the US government. I didn't even know I would be in the infantry.

After just a few days at Fort Sill, we were sent by troop train to Camp Roberts, California, halfway between Los Angeles and San Francisco on Route 101. Our train took the southern route, stopping in Dallas and El Paso, and a lot of other places along the way. At each stop we picked up more trainees until we had twenty to twenty-five cars. Camp Roberts was supposed to be our basic training, but the nation was gearing up for war and had an abundance of raw recruits, but few noncommissioned officers (NCOs) to train them. We didn't see many NCOs at Camp Roberts, and we never had a drill instructor in our training company. We had a little corporal who had been in the service just six months or a year and was less than enthusiastic about gaining responsibility for a company of trainees. He wasn't a proper drill sergeant. We all knew he didn't know what he was doing and had never been trained for the job. He seemed like a decent enough guy, but most of us in the company felt we were short-changed with our basic training. Not that we missed having a proper drill sergeant scream and curse at us, but we all knew there was a good chance we'd have to face the enemy, whether in the Pacific or in Europe, and we wanted to be ready. We didn't see much of our corporal. He'd appear each morning, when he'd tell us what to do or where to go, and again at lights-out, when he made sure we were all in our bunks. Sometimes he showed up to march us to chow. At times he didn't, and then we'd just walk as a company to chow on our own. He never assigned one of us to assist him. I think he hid out most of the time, or maybe he had other duties. In any case, I don't have any endearing memories of my drill sergeant, because in reality I didn't have a drill sergeant.

We were at Camp Roberts for three months, from January until April 1942. Initially, all we did was police up the area (pick up trash and cigarette butts) around our barracks and march to chow. We worked on menial projects for the camp, like spreading crushed rock around the barracks and the rifle range. We were awakened early and had to be in our bunks at 2100. Finally, we started to get some training. By the middle of February we were marching to the rifle range every day, rain or shine. We would be on our way at 0600, practice marksmanship at the range all day, and return to the barracks at night, clean our rifles, and lights out at 2200. We weren't allowed off post, so I saw nothing of the local area.

While I was at Camp Roberts, unbeknownst to me, my cousin Leonard Robinson was fighting for his life in the Philippines, in a four-month battle that resulted in his becoming a Japanese prisoner of war. I knew Leonard was in an Army anti-aircraft artillery unit, as he had been drafted before Pearl Harbor was attacked, and sent to Clark Airbase with the 200th Coast Artillery (Anti-Aircraft). The Japanese attacked the Philippines the day after they attacked Pearl Harbor, and soon invaded the country with ground troops. On April 8, 1942, after American and Filipino soldiers fought a delaying action against the Japanese invaders for four months without receiving any new supplies or help from the States, the American commander, General King, surrendered his entire force on the Bataan Peninsula to the Japanese. Leonard then became part of the infamous Bataan Death March, in which over 5,000 Filipino soldiers and 1,000 American soldiers died, and spent a subsequent three and a half years as a prisoner of war. He wrote of his experiences in a book entitled *Forgotten Men* (Trafford Publishing). As a prisoner, Leonard often provided spiritual comfort and assistance to his fellow prisoners, and after the war became a Baptist minister in Casper, Wyoming, where he lives to this day. He's also a chaplain for the Veterans of Foreign Wars, and travels over a four-state area to perform his duties, which often include presiding at the funerals of veterans. But as I continued my training at Camp Roberts, Leonard's trials were unknown to me, and none of my relatives told me about it until after I returned from the Pacific theater myself. However, the events that so changed Leonard's life would indirectly affect mine too, as his commander, General Douglas MacArthur, fled the Philippines in March 1942, and took up residence in Australia. MacArthur became the Supreme Commander of Allied Forces in the Southwest Pacific Area, and later led the land offensive against the Japanese, which began with the Battle of Buna.

While I was at Camp Roberts, I ran into Leona Nievar's cousin. He was the only person I saw during my army training who I'd known in my civilian days. By the end of January, I was writing to Leona and calling her "Babe." By the end of February I was calling her "My Dear Darling" and "honey" in my letters. I know now I wasn't the only one corresponding with her, but we wrote to each other throughout my tour overseas. When I was in the States playing baseball before the war, I had a lot of girls hanging around the ball park, but I rarely had time for them, since my first love was baseball. However, now that I was in training, I was eager for words from home, and Leona was one of the few people, including immediate family members, who wrote to me. Those letters caused me to think about her a lot more. In response to being asked why she wrote to other military men besides me, Leona later said she was just being practical. It was wartime, after all, and there were a lot of lonely GIs around. In addition to doing her part to keep the morale of the troops up, there was the simple reality that some of those in uniform wouldn't be coming home. It made sense to "bait a few hooks," so to speak, and see what happened. Maybe she married me because I was the one who came home first. I like to think not. I do know she corresponded with a B-17 gunner named Walter who was shot down over Germany and taken prisoner, and sat out the war in a German stalag. I guess that knocked Walter out of the game.

About the middle of March, some of us had hopes of going to Texas for Officers' Candidate School (OCS). I understood that if I did well in training I'd have a chance at OCS. I'd been rated a sharpshooter with the rifle and expert with the Browning Automatic Rifle (BAR). So I, along with a man in our company who'd been an elementary school principal in civilian life, submitted the paperwork necessary to apply. The Army never bothered to reply to either one of us. Also in mid-March Bob Hope came to Camp Roberts. At the time, my company was in the mountains on maneuvers and we didn't return to camp until late at night. When we returned, the famous comedian was gone. We were all disappointed at missing our chance to see him.

Private Robert Freese (left) and two fellow trainees at
Camp Roberts, California, March 1942.

Rumors had been flying since the end of January that we were to be shipped out to Australia. Still, the Army wasn't known for keeping privates abreast of their plans. Without warning, one April evening after chow, we were told to get packed—we were scheduled to move out at 2100 that night. We were ordered to stuff all our uniforms and equipment into a single duffel bag, and loaded up in 2 ½-ton GMC "deuce and a half" trucks. Ten soldiers sat facing inward on wooden fold-down benches along either side of the truck bed, while our twenty duffel bags rested in the middle at our feet. We went from sitting down casually eating our dinner, thinking we'd spend the night in our bunks that night, to arriving in Monterey at midnight, within a matter of hours. By now we were used to doing what we were told, without questioning why. We found ourselves at Fort Ord in Monterey, near the beach. We were ordered into barracks, where we slept like logs until late morning.

In the evening we loaded back up again, twenty to a truck, and convoyed up the coast about 120 miles to San Francisco, reaching our destination after dark. The trucks drove directly into dockside warehouses, our movements taking place during hours of darkness and as inconspicuously as possible to ensure the whole division slipped away secretly. We climbed out of the trucks and formed into columns, which then fed into the bowels of dockside ships. The ships included the SS Monterey, the SS Lurline, and an old German freighter, among others. The rest of the 32nd Infantry Division had already been loaded. It appeared they were all waiting on us new troops. We were loaded by regiment—that's when I found out I belonged to the 128th Infantry Regiment, which was assigned to sail on the SS Monterey. I was relieved, because the Monterey was a former cruise liner, and the berthing was fairly decent. The Monterey and the Lurline (both about the same size - 18,000 tons) were part of the Matson Lines' "White Fleet," which had been converted to pack in 3,500 soldiers each instead of 700 to 800 pampered passengers. Later in the war, they'd each carry at least 6,500 marines per voyage. The Monterey's swimming pool had been emptied of water and filled with ammunition. As I looked around my new accommodations, I saw that there were six of us bunked in a former passenger cabin, and I didn't know the other five men. They were all guardsmen, and they were buddies. I was the odd man out. It was only at that moment that I became aware that I'd been placed with a National Guard division. While I was starting my new life in the Army, a National Guard infantry division from Wisconsin and Michigan was rapidly preparing for action, as it had been called to active duty in October 1940. It was the 32nd Infantry Division, a unit that meant nothing to me until this time, but one I'd later identify with for the rest of my life.

The 32nd Infantry Division had a history going back to World War I, where it earned the nickname "Les Terribles" from the French for its toughness in battle. Its shoulder patch was a red line pierced with a red arrow, symbolizing its success in breaking through the enemy line. So it was now known as the *Red Arrow* Division. It had been the first division to pierce Germany's famed Hindenburg Line. Like many National Guard units, between the World Wars its military might existed mainly on paper. The division's "weekend warriors" trained at local National Guard armories with aging World War I equipment. Then, after France fell to the Germans in June 1940, war loomed on the horizon and the United States began to prepare. Eighteen National Guard divisions were ordered to active duty, the 32nd Infantry Division among them. The division trained for over a year before Pearl Harbor was attacked, with some of the training involving maneuvers in Louisiana. Unfortunately, though Louisiana has plenty of swampland, the division didn't train in the swamps, because they were preparing for deployment to Europe. Then, to their surprise, the division was suddenly ordered to the Pacific in March 1942, to check the seemingly unbeatable advance of the Imperial Japanese army across the Pacific. The entire division had just three weeks to ship out from San Francisco. As they prepared to depart, a significant problem remained. The division was supposed to deploy to Australia with 11,600 men, but had less than 7,000.[1] That's where I came in. As they rushed to fill the ranks of the quickly deploying division, 3,000 active duty soldiers were pressed into their ranks, most of us draftees fresh from basic training. Despite the influx of the additional men, the division was still about 1,800 men short, and didn't have all the equipment needed to deploy.

It was April 22, 1942, when I boarded the SS Monterey. In the four months since Pearl Harbor, I had one month of freedom and three months in the Army. We weighed anchor while it was still dark, and as we sailed out of the harbor, I made my way topside. I stood on the Monterey's deck as we glided under the Golden Gate Bridge, which was well lit despite the war, and watched car headlights traveling across the bridge overhead. It was the strangest sensation. The civilians in the cars above us were completely removed from our reality. I felt an odd loneliness as we cleared the bay and ploughed through the dark sea, into the unknown, leaving our homeland behind. Many on the Monterey would never see the United States again. We weren't leaving on a goodwill tour. We were plunging toward a clash with the enemy, to kill them or be killed. I glanced around me at the youthful faces lining the rails. I wondered who would return home, and who would be killed. Yet, besides those morose feelings, I also felt part of something grand. I was aware of being part of history, part of monumental events that I was now inextricably connected to, and maybe, with many others, central to. I uttered a silent prayer, requesting safety for my comrades and success for our endeavor. Then, there was another emotion stirring within me. It was a form of excitement. I was sailing on a large ship for the first time in my life. I knew I'd see things I'd never seen before. I guess, right then, I was almost having fun; I knew this was probably the biggest adventure of my life.

The first night out, the seas were rough and many men got sick, including many of the sailors. Most of the sailors were unseasoned recruits who, like some of the soldiers, had just completed basic training. The rolling of the ship didn't really bother me, but once in a while during the voyage I felt sick, and would go up on deck, and be alright. A lot of men got sick in the mess hall a few decks down, and the smells, which added to one's nausea, tended to get trapped down there, along with diesel fumes and the strong odor of thousands of sweating, seasick men. I think most of the men settled down and got over their seasickness, but some were sick for the whole voyage. For them it was truly a miserable experience. But for me, it was kind of enjoyable. Our first morning at sea, I watched as dozens of sailors were suspended over the side of the ship on rope seats, and began painting the stark white Monterey navy gray. The ship had originally been painted so white that it stood out in stark relief from the sea. The navy boys painted it gray right down to the water line.

At first, life aboard the Monterey was confusing for me. The men I bunked with were from G-Company, but they showed me no camaraderie, and no officers or NCOs gave me any instructions. They all just sort of ignored me. Since I was one of the new guys, an outsider, I didn't really get to know other soldiers until after we arrived in Australia. The National Guard soldiers just saw me as a new recruit and their attitudes were, "The heck with him." While I did feel like the odd man out, at the same time I was thankful nobody was bossing me around. In a way, I really had it made on the ship. I had complete freedom. I almost felt like a stowaway, except I was going in the wrong direction, away from the USA and toward the front lines. The one person I did get to know was Staff Sergeant Bob Teeples, a tall, dark haired guardsman from Black River Falls, Wisconsin, who was in charge of the headquarter supplies. From him I found out that the 32nd had a ball team. He played shortstop and pitcher, and was also the team manager.

Springfield M1 Garand Cal. .30-06 Rifle

It was on the ship, on the way to Hawaii, that I was issued my own rifle, a .30 caliber M1 Garand, which was the standard issue infantryman's weapon in the US Army. It would be the rifle I used in combat, until it was shot out of my hands in battle. But more on that later.

All I thought at the time was that if I cared for my M1, it would serve me well, and might save my life. I broke it down and cleaned it carefully, wiping each piece clean. It was a good day. As I caressed the smooth wooden stock and put the butt to my right shoulder, closing my left eye and looking down the sight with my right, I wondered where this rifle would end up, where I would end up. I wondered if it would be used to kill another human being. It was supposed to be an infantryman's primary weapon, a tool. A tool used for killing. Still, I didn't think about it too deeply. A merciless enemy had attacked our country, very near where I was at the moment. Our job was to take the fight to him. I felt sure that all of us were prepared to do that.

It took three or four days to reach Hawaii, and we dropped anchor outside Pearl Harbor. Though we could see the harbor and city lights in the distance, nobody was allowed off the ship. We were frustrated to be so close, not only to a beautiful city, but to recent history, and were curious to see the damage our new enemies had wrought. Instead, we sat in a rolling ship, unable to see anything of interest. We could observe the coastline, and Pearl Harbor in the distance, but we couldn't make out any navy wreckage or other damage from the historic battle four months before. Finally, after waiting there at anchor for two or three days, more ships, including one cruiser, joined us, and we weighed anchor and sailed for Australia. The ships in our convoy zigzagged to avoid Japanese submarines, and we could hear our escort ship firing its anti-aircraft artillery guns for practice against air attack. Our cruiser left us shortly before we reached Australia. I understand it participated in the Battle of the Coral Sea, which turned out to be critical in keeping the Japanese from landing on the south coast of New Guinea, and later attacking Australia.

I don't know if I was supposed to or not (as nobody had given me any instructions), but during the voyage I went up on deck whenever I wanted to. As I explored the ship, I realized how good I had it. Many other soldiers were stacked six high in canvas hammocks all over the more open areas of the ship, like the unused ballroom and the bar. The luxurious days of the cruise line were over, at least for the war. I finally discovered why no NCOs in G-Company were bothering me when I found out I really belonged to L-Company. It wasn't until we were a few days from Australia that 3rd Battalion finally sorted it all out and told me to gather my belongings and move to L-Company's berthing area. I eventually learned that I was part of, from the smallest to largest unit: Company L, 3rd Battalion, 128th Infantry Regiment, 32nd Infantry Division. By that time the voyage was almost over and I'd enjoyed a pretty carefree trip.

Our destination was Sydney Harbor on the east coast of Australia, but we were prevented from docking by Japanese two-man subs attacking the harbor. We were forced to sail around the southern end of Australia to Adelaide. We arrived on May 14, 1942. We knew we were getting close to land when the water turned a beautiful light green. I'd enjoyed the voyage for the most part, and wasn't really ready for it to be over. Ahead lay hard training, hard living conditions, and eventually hard battle. But again, I had mixed emotions. Ahead of me lay Australia, a new and wonderful country I was ready to explore. I was just not sure how much Uncle Sam would allow me to see. Now, as I stood on deck on the starboard side, I heard a soldier who'd just come back from the bow tell his buddy standing near me, "Hey, come up here John, you can see Adelaide in the distance." As we pulled into port, I went forward to the bow to witness our entrance. The ships remaining in our convoy spread out to their appointed berths in the harbor. There were no flag-waving cheering crowds, no fireboats streaming fountains of water alongside us, no speeches. We simply slipped into the harbor quietly like any cargo ship arriving that week. As Adelaide wasn't our intended destination, nobody was prepared for us, and as a result we were housed in old chicken coops.

CHAPTER THREE:
AUSTRALIA

Soon after we docked in Adelaide, it became clear my carefree days aboard ship were over, as I was one of 100 soldiers assigned to unload the ship. The benefit of getting stuck with that duty was that I became better acquainted with Bob Teeples, who, as a supply sergeant, had to help with the unloading anyway. Though I knew they'd already formed a team much earlier in the States, I told him I wanted to try out for the 32nd Infantry Division baseball team. Most of the designated stevedores continued offloading the ship, but after two days I left the port of Adelaide to try out for the team, and I made it. I was elated to be in my element again on the ball field and, at least partly, away from the tight constraints of military life.

The 32nd Infantry Division's ball team normally played other Army units or the Army Air Forces (AAF), with most of the spectators being Australians. On occasion we'd play an Australian team, but there weren't many of them. The games were usually played on horse racing tracks. Players changed or whole teams disappeared due to requirements of the war. I remember once playing the navy, and the next time we went up against them, it was a whole new navy team, since there were so many sailors coming and going. Later, we missed the championships when we shipped out for New Guinea.

In Adelaide, when I wasn't playing baseball, I trained on the use of different types of weapons. While I never trained with heavier weapons such as .50 caliber machine guns or mortars, I did gain proficiency on the bolt-action M1903 .30 caliber Springfield rifle (used during World War I), the .30 caliber M1 Garand, .45 caliber Thompson submachine gun (Tommy Gun), .30 caliber Browning Automatic Rifle (BAR), .30 caliber air-cooled machine guns, and grenades. My favorite rifle at the time was the M1, simply because it was more modern (it held more shells than the M1903 and was a semi-automatic), and unlike the Tommy Gun, could handle a bayonet.

At the time we thought we'd have to defend Australia itself, so our Australian trainers passed on their knowledge of the harsh conditions we could expect, fighting in Australia's arid Outback. We'd find rugged terrain, little water, vast distances between populated areas, and many dangerous critters. What we didn't get was training on how to fight in the jungles of New Guinea against a dug-in tenacious enemy.

We were in those Adelaide chicken coops for at least six weeks, and at times it got pretty cold. I was happy to be housed with the cooks, who had access to cardboard boxes. We tacked cardboard up on the inner walls of the chicken coops to try to fend off some of the cold. There was a little stove in our chicken coop, and again, thanks to the cooks, we had access to the skins of sheep they butchered in preparing mutton dishes for the troops. We fed the skins into the fire, which made the stove red hot, so we didn't have to chop wood, like the other troops did, to fuel our stove. Speaking of mutton, our cooks had no idea what to do with it, and tried to cook it like hamburger. Later I discovered that mutton properly prepared by Australian ladies was something else altogether—it was a delicious treat.

The best time for baseball in southern Australia is December through February, as the seasons "down under" are opposite ours, and that's their summer. When we arrived in May the cold weather had already arrived, but when it snowed it would all melt within a few days and we would play ball again, at least until the weather interfered. I'm not going to say we were celebrities, but being on the division baseball team did mean we got a little leeway. The rest of the division trained all day, but the baseball team trained only until noon, then went to practice. Later, during the fighting, I sometimes wished I'd spent more time training for combat and less time playing baseball, but baseball meant more to me than anything at the time.

Halfway through the games we'd take a break for an hour and have tea under the stands. It was sort of like intermission. There'd be other activities for the fans to watch, like tug-of-war contests and so forth.

During the war it wasn't uncommon for GIs far from home to be invited to a home-cooked meal by local citizens, both in the States and in allied countries like Australia. At one of the ball games I met twenty-three year old Molly Stewart, who took me to her parent's home for dinner in the evening. I went out with her a few times and developed a friendship. Years later, after Leona and I were married, Molly sent us a stuffed wallaby and koala bear for our kids. Several times after games, I was invited to dinner by a twelve-year-old girl. The first time she asked I turned her down. It would've been embarrassing to accept an invitation from a child, so I held out for a better offer. During intermission the plucky young lady came back and asked again. That was my last chance, so I accepted. I rode the train home with her and her parents, and as it turned out her father was the mayor of Prospect, a suburb of Adelaide, and she had three married sisters who lived in the family home while their husbands were overseas in the military. Her mother's lamb dinner was the best I'd ever eaten. I didn't have mutton that good again until, many years later, an Englishman named John Pike prepared it even better.

We'd sometimes be in different towns, away from our camp, and would go home with a member of the community to share their Saturday evening meal with them. Being away from "home," we often spent the night, unless there were only women in the home. In which case, for propriety's sake, we wouldn't stay overnight. Australia was different for us culturally in that women at the ball games would come up and invite us to dinner as quickly as a man would. I suspect the GIs who came to the ball games as spectators were treated well, but I can say for certain those of us who represented the division on the ball team were received with quite a bit of hospitality. When we left with "our family" after the game, usually it was just one GI per Australian family, probably because of wartime food shortages. The quantity and quality of the food varied from house to house. At one home for breakfast the hosts might offer coffee and toast, and the next family would lay out a full bacon and eggs breakfast. During away games, if a family fed me but didn't have a place for me to sleep, they'd talk to their neighbors and find someone with room for the night. They were very accommodating. In my mind, the best part of having dinner in Adelaide was that they knew how to cook mutton right.

We normally left camp on Fridays at 1000 for away games, traveling in a couple of Army 2½-ton trucks, and arrived at our destination before dinner. Sometimes we'd arrive in time to have a practice session before dark. Games were Saturdays and Sundays. There were about twenty men on the team, and half of them were pitchers. We went through a lot of pitchers because of the long breaks we had for tea halfway through the games. After a break like that, the pitcher's arm would get cold, and we'd have to go to a new pitcher.

In July 1942, the 32nd Infantry Division moved from Adelaide to Brisbane, halfway up Australia's east coast, a thousand miles northeast of the Adelaide chicken coops. On the way, we played a ball game in Melbourne and two in Sydney, while the division was changing trains. As odd as it may sound, Australian territories used different gauges of railroad tracks. The division's move meant crossing four territories, so there were big delays where the gauges changed. At each change the entire train had to be unloaded, not only of troops, but also of all equipment and supplies. Once unloaded, everything had to be reloaded on a new train, waiting across state lines, so to speak. Happily for me, the delay gave the division team a chance to play ball, and instead of unloading the train, we were taken away to represent the division on the ball field.

Once in Brisbane, ninety percent of our home games were played at the old Eagle Farm Racetrack, which now, in wartime, hosted an Army camp called Camp Ascot, built by the Australian army for the US Army. Camp Ascot was named for a suburb of Brisbane and was home to a fighter squadron, an artillery regiment, the largest hospital in the area, and many other American units. More importantly, as far as I was concerned, it had a pretty good ball field with a diamond and a fence along one end of the track. They spent some money getting it ready for baseball, no question about it. There were no horse races there during the war, so Australians came out by the thousands to watch the Yanks play baseball. Even though Camp Ascot was the team's new home field, it was still thirty miles from Camp Cable, where the 32nd Infantry Division was based throughout the rest of our stay in Australia. Other players tired of all the riding we did in the backs of trucks to get to and from our games, but I didn't mind. It was better than being out in the field training with the rest of the division, and being ordered around by our NCOs.

Camp Cable had been carved out of the countryside only recently, and was sadly given its name the hard way. When we left Adelaide, most of us traveled by train to Brisbane, but some 32nd Infantry Division troops sailed around the southeast coast of Australia in cargo ships. One of the ships was torpedoed by a Japanese submarine, and the only man lost was a twenty-five year old corporal from Michigan named Gerald O. Cable. Thus, the camp was named for the first man in our division killed as a result of enemy action.

Camp Cable was a fairly rudimentary base out in the country, south of Brisbane. Although we had stoves to keep us warm in Adelaide, farther north at Camp Cable we didn't need them. There were no barracks; we set up canvas tents, six to eight men per tent, in the woods. The men either set up their tents under the trees, or where it was too thickly forested, went to work cutting down trees to make room for their tents. I soon fell in with half a dozen other guys from Company L and we set up a tent under a tall tree. With the temperature often around 100 degrees, the seven of us kept the tent flaps open, and frequently rolled the canvas sides up, too. On more than a few warm nights, as I lay on my cot, I'd look up to see a wallaby sticking its head in the tent, looking for food. Sometimes I'd wake up to look right into the eyes of a wallaby staring at me face-to-face. As a smaller version of the kangaroo, its head would be at the same level as mine as I rested on my cot. It was a bit startling. We saw koala bears in abundance down in Adelaide, and with their furry coats they were acclimated to those colder temperatures, but I never saw one in the Brisbane area, perhaps because of the warmer climate. When we were hiking in the bush around Camp Cable we saw snakes and other critters, but happily I didn't come across any snakes in our camp. Probably the strangest animals were the three to four foot long lizards, which made a laughing-like sound, we'd come across when combat training in the woods. These reptiles were creatures from another world to my eyes and ears, but I never knew of any of them biting an American soldier. The lizards must've moved at night, because during the day we'd see them clinging motionless to trees. From a distance sometimes they looked like big knots on the trees.

At Camp Cable, the 32nd Infantry Division finally got into some serious training, but I missed most of it because I was too busy playing center field for the division ball team. For example, once, L-Company was engaged in a twenty-five mile hike, but because I had to be at a baseball game, I was brought back to Camp Cable in a truck by noon. Still, even the division as a whole didn't get much training on jungle warfare back then. In hindsight, one thing the Army should've given us more training on was the bayonet. In actual combat in the jungles of New Guinea, the most useful weapon, hands down, was the bayonet; in battle we mainly used our bayonets augmented with grenades. Though we practiced marksmanship on a rifle range three to four miles outside Camp Cable, in battle we used bayonets far more than our rifles.

There were no sidewalks or wooden walkways at Camp Cable. If it rained, it was muddy. It was all pretty open to the elements. I'm not aware of any plumbing or electricity in the camp. Until much later, there were no chow halls in buildings, except for the officers' mess. L-Company's tents were next to T-Company's, and we ate our meals together nearby in mess tents where thirty to forty men could sit down and eat at a time. We normally had three hot meals a day. For dinner, the cooks ladled out their wretched mutton stew. It was so foul we had to throw out the meat. It stank terribly. For breakfast, we enjoyed eggs and bacon, or whatever the cooks wanted to fix. Those of us on the division baseball team were allowed to use the battalion officers' mess after practice, since the officers' mess was closer to the practice field. That made it harder for me to get along socially with the other men in my company, as I was the only one from L-Company on the team. The other men resented my receiving special treatment. Team members were the only enlisted members who didn't have to be invited to the officers' mess—all baseball players could eat there after practice. Even though we were semi-celebrities, the military discrimination against enlisted personnel still prevailed. The ball players, who were all enlisted, sat together at their own table, separated from the officers.

For entertainment, the Army showed movies on huge sheets or pieces of canvas on the side of a hill. However, given the combat training schedule, most men were tired at the end of the day and hit the sack around 2100 hours. When soldiers did find some leisure time, they spent a lot of time gambling. In that way, some soldiers lost all their hard-earned, and meager, pay. I knew men who'd be broke the day after payday due to their gambling habits. We had one cook who was always broke; he never had any money to go to town. That never made any sense to me.

After we arrived in Brisbane, the Army began paying us in Australian pounds. In 1942, a private made $21 (paid in cash) a month, and that didn't equate to many Australian pounds. There was a cartoon that came out in 1941 poking fun at Army life with a song that went, "For 21 dollars a day, once a month." We did get Overseas Pay, but the Army also deducted many things, like laundry services, from our pay. Thankfully, in 1943 a new pay scale went into effect. A private received $50 a month, with $10 added for Overseas Pay and another $10 a month (or 30 cents a day!) for Combat Pay. A $10,000 life insurance policy was mandated at $6.40 a month, automatically deducted by the Army. In addition, I had some of my remaining pay sent to my folks in Oklahoma City so I'd have something when I returned. I never remember having much money in my pockets. But, of course, being a baseball player helped defray expenses that would normally have come out of my pocket when I was off post, as the Australian people were very gracious to us when we were away playing ball.

After away games, many of the ball players liked to go at dinner in homes where there might be a young lady. I tried to find homes with the best cooks. Oftentimes, we went into town at night after playing ball, socializing with our host family and playing games in town recreation halls. Australians played a lot of cribbage and bridge, and I remember one game they liked in particular, called lawn bowls, where they rolled a wooden ball about the size of a softball down the grass at a smaller, white, target ball. Sometimes we were back to their homes by 9:00 or 10:00 PM, sometimes at midnight. At times I had a say in where we were going, but usually I was just told that we're going here or there.

The Australians were known as heavy drinkers. They consumed a lot of 16% beer, and I observed that some would take a fifth of whiskey in a sack to work in the morning. I soon gained a reputation as one who'd drink alcoholic beverages only in moderation, abstaining from getting drunk. To my surprise, I didn't see the other men on the team getting drunk either. I know many men in the division were just as wild as they could be, so maybe we were just a team of more conservative guys. However, the team members were expected to be good ambassadors of the 32nd Infantry Division, and I think we were. In any case, I'm grateful that, due to the ball team, I experienced many things in Australia that, unfortunately, other servicemen weren't able to enjoy.

I suppose the US military discouraged serious GI relationships with Australian women, as we were there to train for combat and not to get entangled in long-term relationships. I didn't know any American GIs who married Australian women, but then most men didn't get off Camp Cable very often, and really didn't have much money to travel or get out and socialize.

When I was invited to dinner at Brisbane homes, I noticed most of the men present were either older men in the reserves, or younger men who had been injured in the war, veterans back from North Africa with injuries that rendered them unable to fight in the regular army. The reserves had no rifles—they were forced to practice using sticks for rifles. Still, the Aussies were preparing as best they could to defend their homeland.

By this time, Australia, a country of only seven million people, had already been at war for almost three years. They had loyally joined the British Commonwealth in the fight against the European Axis, but that meant their land, sea, and air strength was dispersed around the world. By the time Japan entered the war against the Allies in December 1941, nine Royal Australian Air Force (RAAF) squadrons were serving with the British in the United Kingdom, the Middle East, and Malaya. Major units of the Royal Australian Navy, which then consisted primarily of five cruisers, had just reached Australia after months with the Royal Navy in the Mediterranean Sea and Indian Ocean. As far as ground forces, the Australians only had four divisions of properly trained and equipped soldiers, and most of those were overseas. Australia's home defenses were in a sad state. For example, the total bombing force left to defend Australia was just twenty-nine Hudson medium bombers and fourteen Catalina flying boats. Its fighters were obsolete Brewster Buffaloes, and were in Malaya anyway. RAAF units defending the homeland had no choice but to use Australian-built Wirraway advanced trainers in lieu of fighters, but they were no match for the far superior Japanese Zeros, and so of course tried to avoid any air battles.[1] The Wirraways were used as artillery spotters and for light reconnaissance, and even used to transport small numbers of troops, as I would personally learn. However, in a head-to-head dogfight with Japanese fighters, they'd have been blown out of the sky.

At the time, most Australians thought they'd have to give up part of northern Australia to the Japanese. Just north of the northern tip of Australia was the stepping stone to any Japanese invasion of Australia—New Guinea, and the northern tip of Australia is less than ninety miles from New Guinea's closest point. The basic shape of the island of New Guinea is like a giant dragon, with its head to the left, followed by a thick body, and a narrower tail flowing down to the southeast.

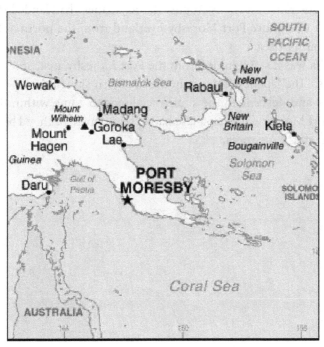

Thankfully, the US Navy's victories in the Battle of Coral Sea (the ocean between northeast Australia and New Guinea) in May 1942, followed by another victory at the Battle of Midway in June, frustrated Japanese plans to capture Port Moresby in the south of New Guinea. Yet the Japanese didn't give up, and instead invaded the northern coast of the eastern tail of New Guinea, with the intention of moving overland across the steep Owen Stanley Mountain Range, south into Port Moresby. With an airfield there, on the south side of the mountains, they'd be in a good position to take further action. While we were training in Australia, the Japanese continued to advance, despite their setback in the Coral Sea.

On July 21st and 22nd, 1942, a Japanese convoy of three transports, two light cruisers, and three destroyers reached Gona, just north of Buna on the north-eastern shore of New Guinea, and 4,400 Japanese troops disembarked. The troops worked their way inland and then southwest onto the Kokoda Trail, a hazardous and meager footpath running north-south over the rugged Owen Stanley Mountains. The Owen Stanley Mountain range runs east-west, and separates the northern, Pacific Ocean, side of the Papuan Peninsula from the southern, Australian, side. By August 11, the Japanese had landed 11,100 men and set out to capture Port Moresby overland from the north, rather than from the south by sea.[2]

Australia was just 340 miles from the Port Moresby area, and that wasn't good news. The Japanese fought up the northern side of the Owen Stanley Mountains and descended the southern slopes to come within thirty-two miles of Port Moresby. The Japanese had to be stopped, or they'd be in a good position to attack Australia.

CHAPTER FOUR:
BATTLING THE ELEMENTS IN
NEW GUINEA

On September 18, 1942, after four months in Australia, we left Camp Cable, traveling by train to York, on the northern tip of Australia. At York, we got all our gear sorted out, checked and ready, and boarded planes for a flight to Port Moresby, New Guinea. We didn't bring much on the aircraft, as there was simply no room. We left our helmets, gas masks, and a lot of other equipment behind. Our regiment, the 128th Infantry Regiment, was to fly. Others were to arrive later by ship.

US T-6 Texan, similar to the Australian Wirraway in
which Robert was transported to Port Moresby.

The plane I was on was small, with room for only six soldiers. It was a single engine plane, I think a converted Wirraway advanced trainer. The rear seat was removed and a cot placed in the middle for us soldiers to sit on. The other planes varied in size; some held fifteen or more soldiers. The US Army used any planes we could get, a mix of Australian and US. Of the six soldiers on our aircraft, five of us were scouts, and one was a lieutenant who wasn't with our battalion, and didn't stay with us. I'm not sure what he was doing there. We sat back to back. Three of us sat on the cot facing the right wing, and three faced left.

Our aircraft was supposed to be the first from the regiment into Port Moresby, but shortly after take-off we experienced engine trouble. As I sat facing to the right, I could look down and see oil streaming down the right wing. The pilot banked to the south and headed back to York. He didn't need to say a word. We saw what was going on, and knew we were returning to our original airfield. It was frustrating for us, and caused a lot of anxiety. Were we going to make it to New Guinea with the others or not? We didn't know how bad the problem was, and wondered if we'd even make it back to the airfield. However, we did make it back to York, landed, and quickly taxied over to waiting mechanics, who began making repairs while we remained in the plane. The pilot told us to just hold tight, and let the air force take care of it. To my surprise, the mechanics fixed the problem quickly, and soon we took off again. On the way to New Guinea, our smaller, faster plane passed all the transport aircraft except one.

As we made our approach into Port Moresby, we saw that the airfield was under attack by Japanese fighters. The US didn't have many fighters in the Pacific at the time and we had no fighter cover that I'm aware of for our mission. We were number two now. The number one plane ahead of us was a twin-engine C-47 transport. They normally flew with a crew of three and up to twenty-eight troops. As it neared the airfield, we watched in horror as a much faster Japanese Zero fighter came hurtling in from above and behind them, hammering away with its two 7.7mm machine guns in the engine cowling and 20mm cannon in each wing. The defenseless C-47 burst into flames and crashed near the edge of the runway. I thought all the poor aircrew and troops on board must have been killed. We passed the burning wreckage as we cleared a mountain just before the runway. I felt sick to my stomach. We had little time to mourn though. After we made it over the mountain and lined up on approach, preparing to land, a Zero flashed by us so close we could see the pilot grinning. It was like a movie. We were suddenly in the war. We knew it was our turn. We knew he would circle around behind us and destroy us at will. I could almost imagine the bullets striking our aircraft, pounding across us, hitting our fragile bodies, the engine, or the pilot, and bringing us down. Maybe those of us in the back would be killed first. Maybe our plane would catch fire and we'd all burn to death as we crashed. Without fighter cover we were sitting ducks. I thought I was going to die before I even made it to New Guinea.

Our pilot didn't want to go down without a fight. He turned around and yelled at us to smash the canopy out and fire at the attacking fighters—we were the plane's only defense. We smashed the canopy with our rifle butts, and held our rifles at the ready while we scanned the horizon for fighters like our lives depended on it. In the end, we touched down without firing a shot. The Zero had somehow disappeared. To this day I'm certain that if that Zero pilot had any ammunition left, he could've and would've blasted us from the sky. Maybe by the time our aircraft arrived the Japanese attackers had used all their fuel and ammunition on the airfield attack, or maybe some friendly aircraft arrived and, unseen by us, drove them away. In any case, that was the first time I felt that God had intervened to save my life during the war.

It turned out that our plane was the first of all the aircraft in the regiment to land. After touch-down, our pilot was forced to taxi left and right around craters left by the recent bombing; for a moment I thought we may have survived thus far only to plunge into a hole in the runway and crash, but we didn't. We were thankful for our pilot's skill. I breathed a sigh of relief for being safely on the ground. Once we landed we realized Australian troops held Port Moresby, for as soon as the air attack was over, they came out to repair the cratered runway and other damage. Until then, I don't think it was clear to the average infantryman whether we'd have to hit the ground fighting or not. The last thing we knew was that the Japanese were very close to Port Moresby and enemy troops had been advancing over the Kokota Trail. As I reflect back on the experience, I'm amazed at how little information was shared with the average soldier. We were normally in the dark on any information the brass had. Thus, we landed in Port Moresby ready to fight, but glad it wasn't necessary.

After our Wirraway came to a stop, the six of us thanked our pilot and climbed out of the aircraft with our weapons and meager supplies. The lieutenant disappeared, and we five scouts went to five different sectors where we were supposed to dig slit trenches and wait for our respective units. It was our job as scouts to lead the way for our companies. I went to my sector on the north side of the runway, dug my hole, and waited. In a short time the men from Company L landed in C-47s and other aircraft. They dug in for the night around me. The next morning we set out to find a way around the Japanese and across the Owen Stanley Range.

Before I describe what our company found, it's worth quoting US Army historian Samuel Milner's book, *The War in the Pacific, Victory in Papua* here:

"The Japanese could scarcely have chosen a more dismal place in which to conduct a campaign. The rainfall at many points in the peninsula is torrential. It often runs as high as 150, 200, or even 300 inches per year, and, during the rainy season, daily falls of eight or ten inches a day are not uncommon. The terrain, as varied as it is difficult, was a military nightmare. Towering saw-toothed mountains, densely covered by mountain forest and rain forest, alternate with flat malarial coastal areas made up of matted jungle, reeking swamp, and broad patches of knife-edged kunai grass four to seven feet high. The heat and humidity in the coastal areas are well-nigh unbearable, and in the mountains there is biting cold. Along the streams, the fringes of the forest become interwoven from ground to treetop level with vines and creepers to form an almost solid mat of vegetation, which has to be cut by the machete or the bolo before progress is possible. The vegetation in the mountains is almost as luxuriant; leeches abounded everywhere, and the trees were so over-grown with creepers and moss that the sunlight can scarcely filter through to the muddy tracks below. The Owen Stanley Mountains, whose peaks rise to more than 13,000 feet, overshadow the entire Papuan Peninsula, running down its center to Milne Bay like an enormous spine."[1]

The Japanese blocked the Port Moresby-to-Buna trail, also called the Kokota Trail, up in the mountains. The 126th Infantry Regiment traveled north from Port Moresby on the Kokota Trail until the Japanese met them in battle and significantly slowed their progress, less than thirty-five miles from Port Moresby. My company was chosen from the 3rd Battalion, 128th Regiment, to try to flank right, farther southeast, to get around the Japanese who were holding the Kokota Trail. The rest of the 128th Infantry Regiment would stay at the Port Moresby airfield, awaiting word from L-Company on the pos-sibility of a route across. It didn't make sense for an entire regiment to go crashing around in the jungle when nobody knew what we'd find. Company L would be the pathfinders for the whole regiment, and I'd be the scout for the company, leading the way at the front of the column. MacArthur wanted a route found around the Japanese, and our job was to find it.

We were issued compasses, but couldn't use them half the time. We were too busy trying to find a way around obstructing vegetation. With few trails, travel through the jungle was more a matter of getting around branches, vines, trees, out of tangled creepers, and up and down steep terrain. The idea of navigating in a straight line was a joke, no matter what it might look like on a map. But then, that was academic, as we had no maps.

L-Company followed a narrow trail for thirty-two miles inland, which turned out to be a few days of wasted effort. The trail did not lead over the mountains. But then, nobody knew what was out there. Not only didn't we know what kind of terrain or natives we'd encounter, we weren't even sure where the Japanese were. Our job was exploratory combat, if need be. We weren't really sure what we'd find.

As we struggled through the jungle, we'd occasionally come across some human habitation. We passed three villages of headhunters, altogether. Most of the women and children were hidden from view, so it was hard to tell how many total villagers there might be, but there were about one-hundred men in each of the first two villages. In the first village I saw four to five rows of shrunken heads strung on poles in rows around a hut. Each head was reduced to the size of a large softball. They were obviously the heads of en-emies from other tribes or villages. There were as many as twenty heads in each row, meaning I was looking at eighty to a hundred human heads. The trail bisected the village, with huts lining both sides. At first I didn't see any villagers. We moved through the village carefully, with half the men point-ing their weapons to the left and half to the right. As the first scout, I was the first to see the headhunters when they came into view. The natives were in the huts or, in the case of huts raised off the ground, under the huts, watching us carefully and tightly clutching their spears. I didn't have to wonder if they were fierce warriors capable of extreme violence—the evidence was hanging from the poles around the huts. I flipped the safety off my M1 and mentally prepared myself to shoot them if it became necessary. If they'd moved in a threatening manner we'd have had to defend ourselves, but they weren't the enemy we were after, and we didn't necessarily feel threatened. Uncivilized as they were, they seemed to know what our rifles were for, and kept a respect-ful distance.

We walked through two villages with headhunters clutching spears. The third village was a pygmy village, where the men blew darts as weapons. These guys seemed even more wary than the others. Some of them had their weap-ons at the ready—small tubes about a foot and a half long held to their mouths, poised and ready to use. We assumed the tubes were loaded with poison darts, and that made us uneasy. We were ready to shoot any of them foolish enough to tangle with a company of US Army soldiers armed with modern rifles. Their village was smaller than the other two, but clustered here and there in a disor-ganized tangle so it wasn't real clear where the trail came out on the other side. It was a little tense getting through the village. However, we slowly and quietly picked our way safely through without incident. In reality, we didn't want any trouble from them, and they didn't want any trouble from us.

In New Guinea, some of the natives were hired by the Allies as porters and proved very useful. However, others were hostile. Some turned western missionaries over to the Japanese, and a number of the missionaries were later beheaded by their captors. Of course we couldn't communicate very well with the natives, but I remember a native we later questioned was asked how many Japanese were in a particular location. He bent down and picked up two handfuls of dirt, then dropped them both. Even without an inter-preter we could translate that one. "Many...many."

Once safely through the headhunter villages, the terrain was steeper with vegetation so thick it became impenetrable. The mountain sides were almost sheer, and we didn't have ropes or any other climbing equipment. We could go no farther, and the decision was made to abandon any hope of this being a way over the Owen Stanley Mountains. As we made our way back from the highest elevations, we came to even thicker vegetation where we had to use our hands to tear at weeds, underbrush, ivies, long grasses, vines, and creepers—a tangled mess—to fight our way through the jungle. We were so poorly equipped for the jungle that we didn't even have machetes. We had to use our bayonets or our hands. With effort, we retraced our steps through the headhunter villages to Port Moresby, weary but a little wiser about what the jungle held for us.

At this point, the Army decided to try something truly innovative for the time; they'd attempt to fly a large number of combat troops to the front in transport aircraft, the first time in US military history such a large force was flown into battle. Thus, after resting at Port Morseby while we awaited the necessary air transport, on October 14, 1942, the entire regiment was loaded into C-47s at airstrips near Port Moresby and flown east, right over the Owen Stanley Mountains, which proved so nearly impenetrable by foot. We landed at a crude airstrip carved out of the kunai grass by missionaries and natives at a village called Wanigela, a prewar Anglican mission site on the northeast coast. The entire 128th Infantry Regiment was thus, in one day, placed much closer to the battle than would've been attained by spending a month or two cutting a trail through the jungle.

US C-47 transport aircraft.

From Wanigela, Company L was detailed out of 3rd Battalion, 128th Regiment, to move toward Milne Bay, more than a hundred miles to the southeast. Our job was to ensure there weren't any Japanese stragglers to the south of us who could get behind the regiment as it worked its way north to Buna, because nobody really knew how many Japanese troops had escaped a recent battle at Milne Bay.

About six weeks earlier the AAF had been brutally attacked at Milne Bay, which would become an important piece of real estate. A beautiful place, on each side of the bay 4,000 foot jungle-covered mountains rise out of the blue-green tropical waters. Between the bay and the mountains lies a narrow coastal strip of swamp, sand, and dense, dripping rain forest. In Allied hands, it would allow the AAF to guard the Coral Sea and Port Moresby against attacks from the east, coming from Rabaul. It would also give Allied pilots a chance to go on the offensive, to hit Japanese shipping and New Guinea bases without being forced to fly over the Owen Stanley Mountains. Also, with some improvements the bay would be made into a resupply staging area.[2]

From August 25th through September 5th, US and Australian combat and support troops fought for their lives against an assault by Japanese marines. The AAF had been building an airfield there, so when enemy troops landed up the coast and tried to overrun the area, there were AAF men, US Army engineers, and Australian soldiers, all thrown together in a desperate struggle with the enemy. It didn't matter if they were Army or Army Air Forces at that point.

We worked our way along the coast and cut trails inland through the jungle, the whole time alert for our first contact with the enemy. We spent seven to ten days pushing through miserable and inhospitable terrain, until we came to Goodenough Bay. Having made it about two-thirds of the way to Milne Bay without seeing a single Japanese soldier, our company commander, Captain Sammy Horton, an original member of the National Guard unit from Wisconsin, decided it was time to turn north and head back toward the rest of 3rd battalion. We didn't have a radio, or any other way to communicate with our battalion headquarters, so Captain Horton probably had instructions to meet them at a certain point north of Wanigela.

Shortly after turning north, we came across a gruesome sight that turned the stomach of every man who saw it and motivated us for the battles we would face later. We were walking near the northern part of Goodenough

Bay when we saw something ahead that didn't look right. As we approached, we saw what was left of a young red-headed Army Air Forces boy who'd been tied to a tree and used for bayonet practice. We knew he'd been dead less than two or three days, because in that extreme heat and humidity meat begins to literally fall off the bones in a matter of days. We guessed that this unfortunate support troop had been captured during the Battle of Milne Bay and brought north by a small group of retreating Japanese. We searched the area but found no sign of the enemy. For all we knew they'd been evacuated from the area by boat, and didn't want to take their prisoner with them. So they tied him to a tree and, from what we could tell, multiple soldiers used him for bayonet practice. This is one reason why so many found it difficult not to hate the Japanese. This experience was deeply ingrained in my mind later when I was ordered to train AAF men who didn't think they needed jungle warfare training. Milne Bay proved them wrong. I never forgot the sight of that young red-headed American and the brutality of the Japanese.

The brutal acts of Japanese soldiers weren't perpetrated by a few renegade officers or NCOs. They were not only condoned, but ordered, throughout the empire. In the book *Japan At War: an Oral History*, Tominaga Shozo, a young university graduate who became a second lieutenant in the Japanese army's 39th Division at Hiroshima in 1941 and went on to fight in China, describes the kind of training officers like him put new conscripts through:

"A new conscript became a full-fledged soldier in three months in the battle area. We planned exercises for these men. As the last stage of their training, we made them bayonet a living human. When I was a company commander, this was used as a finishing touch to training for the men and a trial of courage for the officers. Prisoners were blindfolded and tied to poles. The soldiers dashed forward to bayonet their target at the shout of 'Charge!' Some stopped on their way. We kicked them and made them do it. After that, a man could do anything easily. The army created men capable of combat. The thing of supreme importance was to make them fight…good sons, good daddies, good elder brothers at home were brought to the front to kill each other. Human beings turned into murdering demons. Everyone became a demon within three months. Men were able to fight courageously only when their human characteristics were suppressed. So we believed."[3]

By this time we were just learning of Japanese brutality, now up close and personal, as the Chinese had known for years. Our enemy operated using a very different moral code than we did. For example, in the fight for Port Moresby, Japanese troops fighting their way toward Port Moresby from the north, high in the mountains along the Kokota Trail, got within sight of Port Moresby but then stalled there due to an Australian counteroffensive. When the battle for Guadalcanal forced the Japanese military to divert assets away from New Guinea, the Japanese on the Kokota Trail ran desperately short of food, and actually cooked and ate fellow soldiers who had died of disease, starvation, or battle wounds. Later, advancing Australian troops were sickened to see the remains of Australian soldiers who'd been partially eaten by Japanese troops. The Japanese had tied Australian soldiers to trees, cut strips of flesh from their bodies, and wrapped the strips in large leaves so they could preserve the meat.[4] We faced an incredibly brutal enemy who wasn't playing by any rules we knew. Those who saw the result of Japanese atrocities normally loathed them with a fierce hatred. It was hard not to.

After giving up on finding any Japanese stragglers, L-Company retraced its route to the northwest. At Wanigela we were told that the rest of the battalion had pressed on toward Buna. As we followed their trail to the northwest, off to our right we could see an active volcano spewing lava and fire. We circumvented it, but it was visible for miles.

It was at this time that I first experienced the symptoms of malaria, which remain a part of my life to this day. Normally, people get malaria after being bitten by an infected female Anopheles mosquito. Knowing what sort of environment we'd be fighting in, I'm surprised the Army didn't even come close to having adequate medication available. I alternated between shaking with cold and burning with fever. I was miserable, yet there was no hospital or medical aid station to go to for help. There wasn't anything to do but just keep moving, putting one foot in front of the other. Captain Horton doubled my allowance of quinine—that was all he could do at the time. I was by no means the first one to get malaria either. Others around me exhibited the symptoms before I did.

Quinine masks the effects of malaria, but doesn't cure it. Shortages proved disastrous for us in New Guinea. That's because commercially, quinine was available almost solely from the island of Java, a Dutch colony, and Java was overrun by the Japanese the month after Pearl Harbor. Eventually, we did have an alternative in atabrine, which, ironically, had been developed as a synthetic substitute for quinine by another Axis power, Germany, in the

1930s. A couple of years before the war, the US began a crash program to become independent of foreign sources, so we had a good supply, but atabrine had its drawbacks. It was so new that medical officers were still experimenting with dosage, fearing its toxicity and worried about the negative effects, called atabrine psychosis, it could have. Worst of all, soldiers loathed the taste of it, and most of us didn't think it worked very well.[5] Personally, I thought atabrine was worthless. It didn't do anything for me except turn my skin yellow. And when I took it in hospitals it turned the sheets yellow from my sweat. A full eighteen-day treatment of quinine would mask the symptoms for several months. But MacArthur's army in New Guinea was sorely unprepared for the number of malaria cases, and we either were given just a fraction of the quinine pills we needed, or given worthless atabrine.

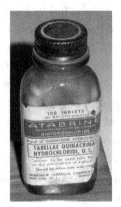

Bottle of atabrine tablets Robert Freese was given at the end of World War II.

It rained day and night and we didn't see much sun. The rain fed small brooks and creeks in the mountains and made very wide and swift-flowing rivers where they joined at the base of the mountains. We came to a river, swollen to about 200 feet across, that we had to traverse. Before we arrived, the Corp of Engineers had strung a strong cable, that the AAF had airdropped to them, across the river, fastening the cable to heavy rods they had driven into the ground on either side of the river. The engineers had secured the help of a lone native who had a dugout canoe with an outrigger on one side to take our company across. The dugout was about ten feet long, and its owner used a paddle at the stern as a tiller. A soldier in the middle of the dugout would grasp a knot tied to a strong rope, which hung down from the cable about three or four feet. Power was provided by the current of the river as a soldier held onto the rope to prevent the boat from floating down the river. It was precarious at best. Yet, remarkably, the whole company got safely across the river. There was only one mishap. When his turn came, one soldier tripped getting into the dugout and fell into the river, but before the current could wash him away two other soldiers pulled him out of the water. It took two days to get the whole company across, three men at a time, though there were less than 100 men left in the company. We had lost about sixty men due to injuries, dysentery, malaria, and other jungle maladies. No matter how badly MacArthur wanted to get the regiments into battle, there was no rushing it. All we had available to us was the one native and his small boat. The division's efforts in New Guinea were already illustrative of how fighting in the Pacific would have its own timetable, a world away from the type of warfare that could and would be conducted in North Africa and Europe. Even to make contact with the enemy, we first had to battle the jungle, extreme conditions, and vast distances from supply and civilization.

Upon reaching the other side of the river, I sat down to wait for the rest of the company. It was good to take a break, but it gave me time to think, think about what it was going to be like when we met the Japanese in battle. I wondered: Would it be a few at a time? Would it be a full company of enemy soldiers charging at us? Or, would we come across each other single file on a trail or in the jungle? Would they see us first and open fire? Would we have enough ammo? What would the rest of the terrain be like—more rivers and thick jungle like this? What about crocs, and snakes? There was no end to the questions flowing through my mind in that lull. My imagination ran wild with the possibilities.

After the company was reunited and started off again, we soon found ourselves mired in the vast swamps of the Musa River delta. For three days and two nights, we were in water as shallow as the tops of our shoes to as deep as our knees—muddy, dirty, grassy, mulchy water. At night we had to tie ourselves in trees to get out of the water and get a little rest. Unfortunately, small green snakes shared the trees with us, and we had to knock them off all night with sticks or our bayonets to keep them away. Giant, oversized lizards looked at us and laughed, or so it seemed. Maybe it was funny to them. I could imagine them thinking, "Why would all these humans willingly plunge into this miserable, dangerous swamp? Shouldn't they be somewhere else?" They grated on our nerves and we didn't get much sleep. There were also blood-sucking leeches, and many of the boys got ringworm, dysentery, jungle rot, and malaria. I certainly had my share. Even worse than being in the jungle was being in a jungle swamp.

Throughout the campaign I saw plenty of giant snakes, about a dozen feet long and six inches in diameter. Unexpectedly encountering one up close in the wild could be a little intimidating to most of the men, but I found if I didn't bother them, they didn't bother me. I would just step over them. We also saw plenty of aggressive crocodiles. When crossing a body of water, one or two soldiers stood guard for crocs, rifles ready, while others crossed to the other side. Many crocs were killed that way. When I was alone, I threw a rock into a creek before crossing, then waited a few seconds to see if any crocodiles surfaced, as they'd think the rock was an animal that had just plopped into the water. I saw a lot of crocs, but didn't end up shooting any. Although we were afraid of the crocodiles, I never heard of a soldier in our battalion being injured or killed by one.

On our third day in the swamp, I was given a note to deliver to the battalion commander, who was farther north. Captain Horton sent me on my way, saying, "Freese, if you run into Japs, you're gonna have to swallow the note… got it?" I said, "Okay, I will." I left Company L and headed north about a day's journey alone. I was able to travel through the swamp much faster than the entire company. I was in good shape, and one man can always move faster than the entire company, which had to wait on the slowest man in the company. All I had was a compass to find my way. No maps were available, but I had a good sense of direction and was told battalion headquarters should be across a creek, which was described. It was impossible to navigate by the sun, as most of the time in the depths of the jungle I couldn't see the sun because too many trees were in the way, and it was frequently overcast and raining anyway. I relied entirely upon my compass.

I experienced a strange encounter during my trek. As I made my way north on a little trail, a brown-haired western missionary boy about ten to twelve years old suddenly came into view, walking toward me. He didn't seem as surprised to see an American soldier as I was to see him. As he wasn't equipped for the jungle, I knew he'd been separated from his family in a hurry. He had clean long pants and shoes, not boots like I'd expect. It hadn't been long since he'd been given a haircut, so I knew he'd only recently been in civilization, more recently than I had been. He acted like he may have known where he was going. To my surprise, he spoke English—he sounded to me like any American boy. He may have been Australian or British, but I don't recall an accent. He said his family had been surprised by the Japanese and he somehow found himself alone in the jungle. I advised him to head due south, as I thought that if he headed north, before long he'd run into Japanese troops. I knew there wasn't anything but swamp to the southeast, as I had just come from there, so I warned him against heading that way. Although he wasn't likely to find any Allied troops (Americans or Australians) if he headed south, at least he might come across a friendly native village, and he did seem to know the area fairly well. I told him he could also wait where he was for the rest of my company to pass by, and follow them north. I advised, "Now there's a whole bunch of men coming up, so you can follow us up if you want to." I never thought about taking him with me, since I was on a mission and had a job to do. The smart thing for him to do would've been to sit there and wait for the rest of the men. Later, when I was reunited with my company, I asked several men if they had seen the boy. They had not, and I never saw, nor heard anything about, the boy again. That experience gave me a lifelong appreciation for the dangers faced by missionaries and their families.

At the end of the day, when I got to the creek, I was relieved to see the rest of the battalion. I was especially happy to be out of the swamp. I was a little surprised that battalion headquarters sentries didn't see me until I got right up to them. Then a sentry shouted, "Halt," and I halted. I informed the guard that I had a message for the battalion commander, and I was immediately taken to him. I was never told exactly what the message was, but I believe the message said that Company L was on its way and to wait in place for them. The headquarters staff fed me and let me rest the remainder of the day until L-Company filtered in.

Once the battalion was reunited, we walked north to Goba on the north coast, and took twenty ton motor launches farther northwest up the coast through the shallow rock-filled waters to Pongani, twenty-three miles from where the Japanese were dug in at Buna. The boats could take twenty-four to thirty men at a time, and I think they belonged to, and were operated by, Australians who had lived there before the war, tending their coconut and pineapple plantations. It was a harrowing journey through the rocky shallows, and not surprisingly to most of us, enroute the boats got stuck on some rocks, so we had to wait for the tide to come in and release us. After the rising tide set the boats free, we made it to our destination with no further drama.

Before we set off from Port Moresby, we were told our equipment would be flown in to us, but it wasn't. For example, we never did get our combat helmets. When I see a photo from the New Guinea campaign, I can tell right away who was in our battalion because we just had fatigue caps. It was understandable though. There was a lot of competition for the limited air transportation available. The AAF did their best.

Even though we weren't well equipped, the missing equipment made little difference anyway. Soldiers in the Buna campaign who arrived by ship and were well equipped at the beginning, soon threw away gas masks, helmets, batteries, flashlights, and even ammunition, due to the weight. In the op-pressive heat and humidity, and with rampant debilitating illnesses, it was difficult to carry much of anything. Most of the men were stripped down to the basics. Each man carried a very small tent, a mosquito net, a compact toothbrush, and a small pack. Every day we would throw a little bit more away. For example, I broke the handle off my tooth brush and threw it away. Every little bit of weight, even half a toothbrush, was an enormous burden in that oppressive heat. Of course we had our rifle, ammunition, and bayonet. Even our shirts, socks, and undershorts rotted off us in a short time because of the rain, humidity, and the creeks we had to cross. When men worked on the beach unloading supplies, they had no clothes on at all. We stripped down to the bare essentials. What we really needed and wanted was food and ammunition, and there wasn't enough of that.

We received most of our ammunition and heavy supplies by sea. Transporting enough equipment to supply a division or more across the Owen Stanley Range was impossible, since there was only a steep, muddy, backbreaking trail from Port Moresby to the front. It took porters, who could carry very little, two to four weeks to make the trip. And of course, the 126th Infantry Regiment, fighting on the Kokota Trail, had to push the Japanese back through the mountains first, up the south side of the Owen Stanleys, and down the north side, before the Allies could even begin using it as a supply route. The same distance could be flown by transport aircraft in just over half an hour, but the planes alone couldn't transport enough to fully supply thousands of soldiers. We simply never had enough aircraft. Of course New Guinea has plenty of coastline, but the problem there was that the treacherous waters were very rocky, and the navy couldn't sail in those shallow waters. So units near the coast were supplied primarily by small boats, and those inland had to depend on supply by aircraft. It was a very tough area in which to fight.

Because of the transportation problems, we were poorly fed. For the most part, we were on Australian rations—hardtack, bully beef, and tea, along with a little rice. Because the constant rain and moisture in the jungle made it virtually impossible for us either to heat rations or boil water, most of us ate the food cold and threw the tea away. The bully beef, corned, preserved Australian beef or mutton, came in large, four or five pound tins. It wasn't only unappetizing, it often had a revolting fish-oil taste that caused some of the men to throw up. Many of the tins had become contaminated. Some had been pierced when they were dropped from aircraft. Others had been left out in the open and had rusted. This contamination, along with the impossibility of sterilizing the few eating utensils we had, and the tendency of the over-sized cans of beef or mutton to spoil before we could eat such a large portion, had its effect. Diarrhea and dysentery plagued most of the battalion. Many of the men had to cut holes in the seats of their trousers, so completely had they lost control of their bowel movements.[6]

Mail didn't reach us very often in New Guinea, but when it did, I received a lot of letters at once. Some letters I received were so torn up they were unreadable. During the battle of Buna I received a cake from my Aunt Harriet that was crushed down to about half an inch thick (even though it was in a tin), and moldy throughout. I was hungry, but not that hungry, and had to throw it out.

CHAPTER FIVE:
THE BATTLE OF BUNA BEGINS

T wo months after arriving in New Guinea—the whole time fighting sickness, disease, the terrain, bugs, snakes, crocodiles, unrelenting jungle, and swamp—we finally arrived in position to attack the Japanese forces holding the Buna area. Two or three days before the battle started, I saw half a dozen Japanese soldiers from a distance. They immediately disappeared into the jungle when we spotted them, avoiding contact. They almost certainly were a reconnaissance party counting the number of American soldiers crossing a bridge. They were the first Japanese troops I saw, though certainly not the last.

On November 15, the commander of the 32nd Infantry Division, Major General Edwin F. Harding, issued the division's plan of attack for the assault on the main body of Japanese troops. The first major US offensive against the Japanese in World War II was about to begin. As far as my regiment was concerned, one battalion was ordered to march along the coast to take Cape Endaiadere, southeast of Buna. Another battalion, which would be held in reserve, was ordered to Dobodura to prepare a landing strip for transport aircraft. Our battalion, the 3rd, was ordered to move on the Buna airfields via Simemi village.

The very next day, November 16, disaster struck. Eighteen Japanese Zeros attacked the 32nd Division's supply boats off Cape Sudest, about eight to ten miles southeast of Buna. These small boats, called luggers or trawlers, were carrying vital ammunition, rations, radio supplies, 81mm mortars, .50 caliber machine guns, and equipment and personnel from the 22nd Portable Hospital. Major General Harding was on board, as he had gone on an inspection trip after issuing orders for the attack the day before. Brigadier General Waldron (the artillery commander), a number of noncombatants (including a re-porter, photographer, and two visiting colonels from the United States), and others were also on board. The American troops tried to fight off the Zeros with their rifles and .30 and .50 caliber machine guns, but weren't successful. Soon the boats were burning. When the ammunition began to explode, ev-eryone who was able dove into the water. The two generals made it to shore safely, but twenty-four men were killed, and nearly a hundred were wounded. Two much needed artillery pieces, almost all our incoming ammunition, and the heavy weapons for our regiment, plus the little supply fleet of three lug-gers and a captured Japanese barge, were lost.[1] This single action hurt us tre-mendously. The barge in particular was vital to moving supplies in from the larger ships offshore, as deep draft vessels couldn't navigate the rock-strewn coastal waters. We'd pay a price later in a critical lack of supplies.

I wasn't close enough to see the attack, but I heard it happening. Later, I learned my buddy Bob Teeples was there. He was doing his job, unloading supplies from the small boats, when his boat was attacked and caught fire. With the others, Bob had to leap into the water and swim for his life. I'm sure he had a rough time, because I know from experience that being in the water when a mortar shell, artillery projectile, or bomb hits nearby is about the worst place to be. When the explosion occurs, even if the shrapnel doesn't hit you, the concussion travels through the water easily, and seems to take all your breath away. The concussion alone can damage internal organs or kill. When Bob Teeples finally made it to shore, he scrambled for the safety of the jungle as the Zeros continued their strafing runs. Once Bob realized the attacking Japanese aircraft had departed, he waded back into the water to help care for the wounded. Rescue parties saved many who would otherwise have died.

The loss of the boats was a catastrophe, but the attack wasn't called off. Our artillery pieces, mortars, machine guns, and other essential materiel, which would take weeks to replace, had been lost on the very eve of the Allied attack. The whole supply plan for the operation against Buna was disrupted.[2]

In the absence of resupply by sea the AAF frantically tried to drop us enough supplies, primarily without parachutes. The AAF would kick the supplies, like bags of rice or tins of bully beef, out of C-47s. Often, invaluable food would burst open upon hitting the ground. We existed on rice for quite a while. I call it "swamp seed" and don't care to eat it to this day. At times, all we had for days was whatever coconuts we could scavenge. We learned to soak them in water to soften them up, and then used sticks to dig out the meat from the husks. Apparently I didn't eat as much coconut as rice, because years later I enjoyed showing my children how to crack open a coconut, and then we'd eat it together.

The day after we lost our incoming supplies in the air attack, the Japanese landed 900 fresh troops, from a unit skilled in jungle warfare. Many of these soldiers were from the 229th Infantry, which had fought in China, Hong Kong, and Java. Their two sister battalions were currently fighting on Guadalcanal. All 900 men were deployed in the Cape Endaiadere-Duropa Plantation area, a short distance from us. We didn't know it at the time, but Allied Intelligence had seriously underestimated the number of enemy troops near the coast, maintaining that the Japanese had 1,500 "effectives," when, in reality, we were facing approximately 5,500 fighting men.[3]

On the eve of battle, I was promoted to sergeant, for the first, though not the last, time. Our company had not even made it into combat, and yet had lost many of our officers and NCOs. I was to lead about two dozen men into combat. I had no qualms about that—for some reason I felt comfortable taking on the responsibility. I knew God was with me, and I did a lot of praying. At least every couple of hours, I'd find myself offering silent prayers to my Savior. When the bullets started flying, I thought it was about my time to die, so I was motivated to get to know my Creator a little better. I was sorry I'd wasted so much time before getting serious about my faith.

As our D-Day, Thursday, November 19, 1942, dawned, my 3rd Battalion, 128th Infantry Regiment, was in position at Simemi, about four or five miles northeast of Dobodura (which would become a significant AAF airfield).

We knew we were close to the enemy. We knew we were finally going into battle. It rained hard all day. Not only were we soaked to the skin, but the rain meant we'd have no air support. Unlike D-Day in France a year and seven months later, we weren't fresh troops going into battle. We'd already spent two months in the jungle and were exhausted, dirty, ill-equipped, and sick. After the two mountain guns we had fired a few rounds, our battalion commander, Lieutenant Colonel Kelsie Miller, led us north. Our job was to take the two airstrips southeast of Buna near the coast. They were simply called Old Strip, and less than a mile to the southeast, New Strip. We were also ordered to take the bridge that crossed a creek between the two strips.

These two airfields, found in open ground southeast of Buna Mission (the former Australian government compound), were the most important objectives of the entire Allied drive. The northern airfield was the primary one, originally built years before by the Australians, and recently enlarged by the Japanese with dispersal bays for aircraft parking. The southern airfield was actually a decoy airfield built by the Japanese to try to get our bomber crews to think it was the real airfield and waste ordnance bombing it. But the Japanese had used the dummy airfield operationally as well until the end of September when our air force had cratered it with bombs and put it out of commission. The main airstrip was 3,900 feet long, thirteen football fields end-to-end. In the jungle, that much cleared land was a precious asset. It was just 105 air miles from Port Moresby and 400 from the main Japanese base at Rabaul. Once captured by the Allies, US planes based there could definitely block any Japanese attempt to land at Port Moresby and the Japanese could forget about invading Australia. Later, it would be an important base for the Allied advance up the north coast of New Guinea.[4] We had to take it.

The attack began at 0700. Because the Japanese had destroyed our incoming supplies, we only had one day's supply of food and ammunition. We attacked anyway. As 3rd Battalion approached the trail junction between the Old and New Strips early in the morning, we saw that the Simemi trail petered out to become a narrow raised path, with swamp on either side. Everything was quiet. Then the signal was given by Captain Horton, and the lead platoon rose up and attacked straight toward the Japanese positions, trying to get through an open area about 300 yards south of the junction. They were immediately met by horrendous fire from the western end of the first airstrip (New Strip), from behind the bridge between the airstrips, and from machine guns in front of the junction itself. Twenty-nine men in the lead platoon were wiped out. I felt like they'd walked right into a trap. The lead scout was the only one who wasn't killed. That's because the Japanese waited until he crossed the bridge before opening fire. That was a pretty common method of ensuring gunners killed as many men as possible. If they had shot the scout first, the men behind him would've scattered, so they waited until the main body of troops was close. As that first platoon was being annihilated by machine gun fire, those of us behind them ran off the raised trail and plunged into the swamp on either side. Bullets were zinging all over the place and we began receiving heavy mortar fire. When the rounds impacted the swamp around us, shock waves went through the water and stunned us. We were trapped in open swamp about hip or chest deep, while the Japanese were on solid ground, safely in their pillboxes, which were hidden in the vegetation. We didn't have a chance; they stopped our advance cold. We had to try to withdraw back out through the swamp. Later in the day, as I realized I'd made it out alive, I thanked God and asked Him to be with me the rest of the day. I couldn't even begin to think of tomorrow. I just took each day at a time. I was sure my hours on earth were numbered.

That first day of attack, we encountered a well-hidden Japanese 3-inch naval gun, with the barrel just sticking out near the ground. It was firing at point blank range. The gun was so well hidden that the AAF never did find it, so they weren't able to help us take it out. Later it would be a real problem when tanks arrived, as it fired directly at them like a big anti-tank gun.

We were told that the ground would become less swampy as we got closer to the Japanese defenses, but nobody really knew where we could expect to find solid ground. We had to discover that for ourselves. We had no maps whatsoever. That made coordination between the AAF and the Army very difficult. It was very, very hard for the air force boys to distinguish features in the jungle, or where the Japanese or Allies were. Other problems were weapons related. We had no mortars, and a large percentage of our grenades failed to explode. The Australian Mills bombs (hand grenades) were no good when wet. And New Guinea was usually wet. One of our battalion's patrols stalked the enemy to within grenade range, then threw seven grenades into the midst of a group of ten to twelve Japanese, only to have all the grenades fail to explode. The patrol suffered about thirty percent casualties from return grenades. In addition, we were low on .30 caliber ammunition and had to get more airdropped. Due to the layout of the battlefield, we were forced to attack through swamp, which at times was waist and chest deep. Of course, in conditions like that, it was impossible to carry anything but light weapons, even if we had access to heavier weapons. At the end of that first day, we were still at the edge of a clearing south of the junction. Third Battalion had suffered heavy casualties, and had little to show for it. The next day, pinned down on a narrow front, out of rations, and with nearly all our ammunition expended, we once again made no progress at all.[5] Not a good start to the big attack. It looked like it would be a long battle.

Before we engaged the Japanese near Buna, most of the men, from the top generals down to the privates, thought just getting into position would be the hard part. The AAF had flown over the Buna area for some time and had little to report. Everybody thought there weren't many Japanese troops in place, and we had no idea how well they were dug in. Our perception of the number of Japanese we'd face and the difficulties ahead changed immediately after the attack began. In the midst of the thundering enemy fire, I thought, "Somebody's wrong!" We'd received word two or three times that there were just a handful of Japanese at Buna. Now we thought there must be thousands. And there were. We also thought the Japanese were supposed to be small, but at least some of the enemy we faced were Imperial Japanese Marines, and they were big guys, well trained, well equipped, and well dug in. A formidable foe.

To make matters worse, the overall commander, General Douglas MacArthur, seemed detached from the battle we were fighting. He stayed in Australia the two months we were thrashing around in the jungles and swamps of New Guinea getting into position to attack the Japanese, and only on November 6th did he move his headquarters from Brisbane to Port Moresby. Even then, he chose as his headquarters the comfortable Government House, where the Australian colonial governor had lived, and had it refurbished to his liking. It was probably the only modern western-style building in New Guinea, complete with modern plumbing, fine furniture, and even a library. MacArthur enjoyed hearty meals and a staff of nine native boys wearing serving gloves and pressed white lap-laps decorated with blue stars and red stripes. Not exactly an example of shared hardships with his men. MacArthur sat back in the comfort and safety of Port Moresby issuing orders, demanding rapid attacks and quick victory. Later in November,

MacArthur sent the 32nd Infantry Division commander, Major General Harding, a message that read, "Take Buna Today At All Costs. MacArthur." We were up against thousands of concealed, well dug-in Japanese troops. We had virtually no artillery or tanks or any other means of breaching the Japanese bunkers. A huge swamp limited the division's mobility. The luggers and trawlers that were supposed to resupply us had been sunk, and the Dobodura airstrip wasn't fully functional. The men were filthy, sick, and exhausted after fighting the New Guinea jungle and swamp for two months. General Harding ignored MacArthur's order.[6] Later, General MacArthur removed Harding from command, in our view, for looking out for his men and insisting that they not be slaughtered in nonsensical waves of attacks against prepared bunkers, when we lacked the tanks and artillery needed to pierce the Japanese defenses. MacArthur thought Harding wasn't aggressive enough. Ironically, later in the battle MacArthur's new 32nd Infantry Division commander, Major General Robert Eichelberger, was successful only after he received the tanks and artillery that General Harding had demanded. While after the battle many men respected General Harding for conscientiously ensuring we weren't sacrificed for what we saw as MacArthur's ambition, at the time the politics were way above my pay grade. I wasn't aware of any of the drama the brass was involved in. I had my own problems.

On the third day, November 21, an attack was planned that promised to be better supported. A-20 and B-25 twin-engine medium bombers started off the morning by knocking out a few enemy machine gun emplacements, but they also bombed some of 3rd Battalion's troops, killing four. Worse yet, our battalion commander, Lieutenant Colonel Miller, wasn't told when the ground attack was supposed to begin, so the air support was wasted. The AAF was then rescheduled for 1245, with the air attack to be followed by a barrage from the small number of artillery pieces and mortars the regiment had. We were to begin the infantry attack at 1300. More communication problems ensued, with the result being that the AAF didn't show up. Again, the infantry attack was called off. Finally, at 1600, A-20s and B-25s returned to our area. Most of the aircrews couldn't find their targets, and, disastrously, one B-25 bombed 1st Battalion by mistake and killed six American soldiers. Finally, at 1630 our battalion surged forward. At first we made good progress, but intense Japanese fire soon pinned us down. Forty-two members of 3rd Battalion were killed, wounded, or missing in the attack, for little gain.[7]

The Battle of Buna was only three days old, and I'd already seen plenty of the carnage and confusion war brings. We'd already lost a lot of men. Most frustrating were the mistakes our leaders were making. The joint air, artillery, and infantry attacks weren't well coordinated. We didn't have the artillery or armor we needed to blast through the Japanese defenses. We had no maps, little food, and our ammunition was almost gone. None of these were failures of the common soldier. Even the officers could be forgiven though, if we remember that as a nation, jungle warfare was new to us, plus most of the nation's warfighting resources were devoted to defeating the Nazis first. This was very early in the ground war against Japan. The United States was the newcomer; Japan had been at war for eleven years, since September 1931. The lessons we learned the hard way in the Battle of Buna would pay dividends later. The troops following us in 1943-1945 were much better equipped, with tanks, flame throwers, bazookas, mortars, artillery, and plenty of grenades.

After those first few bloody days, our battalion left one company to keep pressure on the enemy at the bridge between the two airfields, and the rest of us quietly repositioned east to the coast, where we could try to advance on the firmer ground of the narrow beach. The Japanese countered by placing hundreds of snipers in coconut trees on the Duropa coconut plantation, to sow confusion and delay our approach.

One morning, as we slowly advanced, snipers began wreaking havoc throughout our ranks, slowing us down. Now that we were more in the open, it was easier to walk, but we were also more vulnerable. The snipers were harder to see, because the Japanese Type 97 sniper rifles had long barrels and used relatively small 6.5mm shells, which meant the propellant completely burned up before the bullet left the muzzle, so there was no flash. The snipers seemed to take aim at GIs' stomachs, trying to get a gut shot, which would cause enormous suffering and tie up others trying to get the helpless man out of danger, and to medical care. It seemed as if they used a gut-shot man as bait, as his cries would bring brave comrades exposing themselves to hostile fire to get him out of danger.

I was lying in the grass and dirt, trying to get a bead on the snipers with my rifle. To my left, lying on the ground in the prone position, side by side, were two machine gunners, one feeding the ammo belt, and the other spraying the trees and the general area with bullets from a .30 caliber air-cooled machine gun. Suddenly a mortar shell exploded nearby, and both gunners were stunned or wounded. I suspect they were hit by one of our own mortars. At times the propellant got wet, causing a round to fall short of its intended target. I wasn't hurt, so I leaped over the two wounded men and took over the machine gun. I began firing it, like them, lying in the prone position, to minimize my exposure to the snipers, until the barrel got too hot. I used up one belt of ammunition, then reloaded and fired through a second one. I saw bits of bark and leaves flying off the trees downrange. As I fired the machine gun at the tree tops, I saw several Japanese snipers fall out of the trees. Some gave a light "thud" when they hit the ground. Others had tied themselves to the trees with rope, and now hung upside down or at odd angles. Many US weapons were being fired, including another machine gun. I fired the machine gun so long that when I stopped the barrel was bent. I can't say for sure I was the one who killed the snipers, since bullets were flying in all directions. That's okay with me. I'm just as happy not to know.

Our jungle environment certainly affected how we fought. Many times in the jungle there was so much confusion, and it was so hard to see anything, that we didn't know at whom we were shooting. There were times when Allied troops were shooting at each other. Our visibility was limited, and we rarely had a clear target, since the Japanese were so well hidden.

We couldn't throw grenades like we did in training either. Trees, vines, bushes, and other thick vegetation obstructed any long throw, but also, because of all the vegetation, the enemy was close. We had to learn to flip our grenades. We'd just flip them a short distance. We also had to look at the markings on the grenades, which indicated the fuse setting, the number of seconds we had before the grenade exploded. We'd hang onto the grenade just long enough that the enemy wouldn't be able to throw it back before it exploded.

We didn't fight the same way every day in the jungle. Today we might try a route this way, and get stuck in thick jungle or swamp, and the next day we or another company would try another way, maybe along the coast. The Japanese were on pretty solid ground, and well dug in. But the Allied units were mixed up, spread out, and stuck in swamps and jungle, an unfavorable situation for the Allies. It was much easier for the Japanese to quickly support one side of their lines or the other. They were on solid ground in the main habitable areas of Buna, but for us to go even a short distance was very difficult, due to areas of impenetrable jungle and swamp. The Japanese could reinforce their weak areas in minutes. To move the same distance for us would've taken days or weeks. Therefore, each engagement was a separate small campaign of its own.

The Japanese picked the right place to dig in. During the first twenty-six days of the battle for Buna, we probed the Japanese positions, and were fortunate if we could just determine where their bunkers were. It was a costly form of reconnaissance. The jungle closed in on us on all sides. Tactics for maneuver warfare involving companies, battalions, regiments, brigades, and divisions would win battles in the European Theater, but they had no meaning in New Guinea. Often cut off from the other elements of the regiment by the thick jungle and crawling on our stomachs in mud with no visibility around us, each one of us fought his own personal battle.

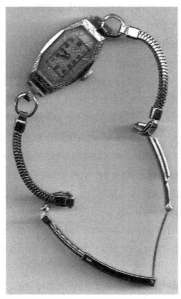

Elgin watch Bob Freese took off a dead Japanese soldier.

One of the first things I picked up as a battlefield souvenir was an Elgin woman's watch with a pearl-like face on it. I took it off a dead Japanese soldier. I suspect he stole it from an American nurse in the Philippines. Many enemy soldiers were veterans of the invasion of the Philippines. I still have the watch, though it doesn't work and I can't get it fixed. I've tried two or three times.

We had to quickly teach the Aussies operating near us some jungle warfare techniques. These were the same Australians who'd stopped the Germans at Tobruk in North Africa (Libya) in 1941, but that fighting wasn't anything like fighting in the jungle. We took small groups into no-man's land and taught them what we'd learned. One day, one of our privates took out a few Aussies for this purpose and saw several enemy pillboxes. He made it back to tell our officers about it, but they refused to believe there were really as many as there were.

The fight for Buna involved a lot of Japanese dugouts or bunkers. However, these weren't dug into the ground and surrounded by concrete like in Europe. Since the water table was so close to the surface, the Japanese troops could only dig shallow trenches. The rest of their fortifications were above ground. They cut down long, straight coconut trees, using them to build log walls. Then they filled empty fifty-five gallon drums or ammo cans with dirt and lined the inside of the dugouts, covering the bunker with a roof of more coconut logs. Everything was topped with dirt and vegetation. With the amount of rainfall that area of New Guinea received, the vegetation quickly grew up around the bunkers, and these nearly impenetrable defenses soon blended right into the jungle. There'd be long rows of these fortifications. The Japanese built two, three, or four, then another row behind, for defense in depth. They didn't exactly have tunnels between them, but they had covered slit trenches they moved through unseen from one to the next. We needed tanks to destroy these pillboxes, but for some time we didn't have any.

One of L-Company's men, a private from McAlester, Oklahoma, was caught in no-man's-land between US and Japanese forces after an attack, and, realizing that exposing himself would mean certain death, spent the daylight hours hunkered down on the jungle floor without moving. He returned to our lines under cover of darkness and warned us of the Japanese bunkers ahead. The next morning, at around 0700, the hungry men of L-Company climbed out of their water-filled foxholes and charged the Japanese positions again. Fire from the Japanese bunkers was intense, with machine gun and rifle fire zipping all around me. Thanks to the man from McAlester, we knew where the enemy bunkers were, but we still didn't have any heavy weapons with which to knock them out.

As we moved forward fifteen or twenty yards, men I knew well fell to my right and left. Suddenly, there was a loud "crack!" that reverberated right through me, and my M1 Garand seemed to explode in my hands. It took a couple of seconds, as my heart raced, to realize what had happened. For a second I thought I'd been shot. But then I realized an enemy bullet had struck the middle of my rifle, breaking the stock in half. The only thing that kept me from being killed by that bullet intended for me was the rifle in my hands. God had chosen to spare me a second time. Fragments of the bullet, or metal from the rifle's trigger guard, impacted my left thigh, but there was no time to examine the wound. My adrenaline surged and I was completely focused on the task at hand. I wasn't thinking much of anything at the time but, "Get me outta here!"

All my actions happened quickly, without much thought on my part. I was single-mindedly focused on one thing. Get another weapon and keep moving. If I remained in one place I was a stationary target, a dead man. Bullets were zipping and zinging all around; I was still getting shot at. A bullet smacked into a tree a foot to my right, spraying splinters and bits of foliage over me. A man from my platoon surged from behind me, past me on my left. Out of the corner of my left eye, I saw his head suddenly snap back and his body fall backward in a heap. I ran over a few steps and saw that he was dead. I picked up his Tommy Gun and pitched forward onto my belly a few feet in front of his body, then half-rolled onto my left shoulder, raised up slightly and aimed the Tommy Gun in the general direction of the Japanese machine gun fire. I squeezed the trigger. Nothing. Rolling onto my back, I slipped out the twenty-round magazine and quickly checked it. There were still bullets in the magazine. I slapped the magazine back in and cranked back the bolt with my right hand to ensure a bullet was chambered. I rolled onto my left side again, aimed, and pulled the trigger. It still wouldn't fire. I threw the Tommy Gun down—it was worthless to me. Getting to my feet and taking a few steps forward, I spotted another rifle, an M1 like mine, lying in a tangle of jungle vines and leafy bushes. Someone who'd been wounded or killed and taken away by the medics must have left it behind a day or two ago in an earlier attack. This one too failed to fire. I ran a few yards to the right, bending almost double to make as small a target for the Japanese gunners as possible, and saw a trusty old M1903 bolt action WW-I vintage rifle lying next to a dead private. I fell to one knee as I picked it up, put it to my right shoulder, aimed it at the enemy bunker, and fired. "Boooom." It worked great, and

I ran forward with it, continuing the attack, pleased to see the bayonet was already fixed on the end of the barrel. Along with the remaining men in our company, I moved forward a few yards at a time, rising slightly and firing, then going back to cover, and repeating. I was glad the M1903 used the same .30 caliber ammunition as my M1, because I still had about twenty to thirty M1 rounds on me. The enemy fire was so intense that our attack soon faltered, and we received the order from Captain Horton to fall back. We'd run right into the Japanese bunkers, and we had no way to pierce their lines with only our rifles and a few grenades. We crawled back about thirty yards while under fire, and dug in as best we could. Our attack had gained less than fifty yards. However, I'd be very satisfied with my new M1903, as it was the most reliable weapon in these taxing conditions. I kept it the rest of my combat tour.

Springfield M1903A3 Cal. .30-06 Rifle

The two worst weapons for jamming in New Guinea were the BAR and the Thompson submachine gun. The filthy swamp water, frequent rain, humidity, dirt, rotting vegetation, and all the other conditions we put up with were very hard on weapons and we didn't have cleaning equipment in the jungle—we barely had food, clothing, and ammo. The M1903 bolt-action rifle was the most dependable in those conditions. Gas chambered (semi-automatic) weapons were often trouble. Even the most famous US infantry weapon of WW-II, the M1 Garand, jammed frequently in New Guinea.

Supplies were so tight that at one point I went for days with just three bullets for my M1903. I had plenty of chances, but didn't fire those last three because I had to save them for when I was most desperate, even though we were attacking every day. And, of course, all the men thought they had to save one last bullet for themselves. We would never allow the Japanese to capture us—that was a fate to which none of us would ever submit. But some of the men didn't have any shells at all. We used our bayonets, the most effective weapon in those close quarters. The proper way to use a bayonet is to, of course, fix it to the end of your rifle, then lunge forward and plunge it into an enemy soldier, then pull up (or down), and twist. It is you or your foe. There was no survival without some amount of brutality. It was a savage way to fight a war, almost as if the modern age didn't exist. All the modern machinery of war used to great effect on the battlefields of Europe was almost useless, and for the most part unavailable anyway, in the jungles of New Guinea. It was a most barbaric, ancient form of struggle; man versus man. Trees, vines, bushes, and thick foliage of every sort inhabited our world in nightmarish quantities, all of it dripping with rain—the jungle itself ensured the fighting would be close.

One problem with our trusted bayonets was that we had no way of sharpening them in New Guinea, and they'd been issued with some sort of hard plastic coating. They just weren't sharp enough. Of course, as I learned, they could still be plunged into a man and do the job. But sometimes when I bayoneted an enemy soldier in the ribs or other bony parts of his body, I wasn't able to pull my bayonet out again, even after stepping on his body with one of my boots and pulling hard on my rifle. I'd leave it in him, release it from my rifle, and go look for a new bayonet. They weren't hard to find on the battlefield with so many men killed or wounded.

I also used my rifle butt to club enemy troops. It was real up close and personal fighting, very primitive. Sometimes, the Japanese would come out of their trenches and pillboxes and attack us at night. We had to be alert all the time. When they came at us like that, they also had bayonets fixed, and we fought close, vicious, combat, man to man. In those circumstances, we used our bayonets almost exclusively. We were afraid if we fired our rifles, we'd hit one of our own men in the dark. I don't know why the Japanese attacked with bayonets at all, as they were protected by bunkers and would've been a lot safer waiting in them for us to attack. In addition, after we took Buna, after it was too late for us to make use of them, I found a Japanese storage bunker with stacks of rifles and ammo several feet high. It looked like the rifles had never been used, and there was so much ammo we took it out and practiced shooting coconuts with the Japanese rifles. However, since the Japanese snuck in replacements continuously on the coast, these rifles may have arrived later in the battle with, and for, their new troops. We found the Japanese rifles were longer than ours, with a smaller, 6.5mm, bullet, and a shorter bayonet, rounded like a spike.

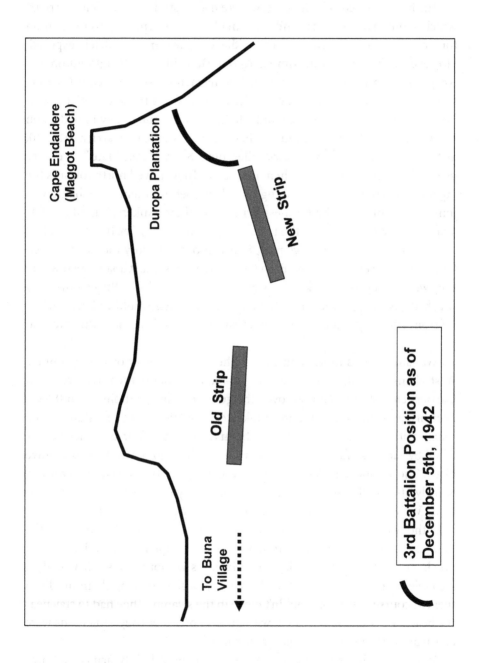

The first armored vehicles we saw were five Australian Bren Gun Carriers, which some may consider similar to small tanks, except they were open on top, meaning from the chest up the soldiers inside were completely exposed. However, Bren Guns were similar to our .30 caliber BAR light automatic weapons, with thirty-round detachable magazines, so Bren Gun Carriers were nothing like tanks. They were just small, light tracked vehicles with no roof that carried some men and a light machine gun. They joined us on December 5th. There were four soldiers in each Bren Gun Carrier. At 0830, as they clanked by us, the crews called out, "See ya later, Mate." We were glad to see them and greeted them in return. They moved north towards the Japanese positions, with us taking our places behind them. The battle was joined, not only with the Japanese firing from their bunkers, but quite a few snipers firing from high in the trees. Twenty minutes after the Aussies had called out to us as they drove past, fourteen of the twenty men in the Bren Gun Carriers were dead. The Bren Gun Carriers were just abandoned where they were. They looked like they were still operational, like they hadn't been touched. No one dared man them as the new men would've been picked off from above by snipers. The vehicles were unusable because they were so open.

We laid down suppressing fire on the Japanese positions as two brave Australians, one officer and one enlisted man, ran out to the three Bren Gun Carriers closest to us and removed the guns and ammunition. Then the officer ordered the enlisted man to take cover, while he ran out alone to the fourth with a Tommy Gun. Before he made it to the fourth carrier he was felled by Japanese fire. We were sorry to see him go down; he was a brave man. The Japanese ended up getting the guns out of the last two carriers. Shortly after 1000, after gaining less than forty yards, our advance stopped cold. We were pinned down by an enemy strong point made of logs, located near the water's edge. The events of that day, December 5, convinced the new 32nd Infantry Division Commander, General Eichelberger, that we had no chance of breaching the Japanese defenses without tanks.[8] It would be a couple more weeks before the US Army was able to bring them in. Even then, of course, our tanks couldn't move in the swamp. They had to stay near the beach, or could be operated, with great effort, after rough log roads were constructed through the jungle by engineers.

With the rather rude lesson we'd received about lightly-armed infantry versus hardened bunkers under our belts, we were now ordered to patrol in small groups and feel out the enemy, while we continued to harass him. Our commanders would order no more foolish frontal attacks without sufficient armor or artillery. We settled into somewhat of a siege mentality while we waited for the big guns to arrive.

By December 7, the first anniversary of the attack on Pearl Harbor, I was very sick with malaria and had a temperature of 103 degrees. Captain Horton gave me permission to walk ten miles back to the 2nd Field Hospital at Simemi. When I arrived, the medical staff wouldn't allow me to stay. They said my temperature had to be 104 degrees before the hospital would take me. I didn't know it then, but their refusal to admit me saved my life—a life lesson for me, that I shouldn't get angry when things don't seem to go my way. God can see the bigger picture, but I can't. The field hospital staff gave me six quinine tablets and told me to walk back to the front lines. Before I left, I visited with some of my buddies from the division baseball team lying in cots in the field hospital. We had a nice, but short, conversation. Then I left for the front. I don't know how I walked twenty miles altogether with that fever.

32nd Infantry Division baseball team before combat in New Guinea. Robert Freese, front row, lying down. Most of these men were killed or wounded during the Battle of Buna. Only three would return to duty in Australia.

That night, three Japanese navy dive bombers and eighteen Zero-escorted high-level bombers attacked the hospital I'd just left, and six of my friends from the ball team were killed. I don't know how many medical staff and other soldiers were killed. We heard about the bombing the next morning, when our company runner returned from battalion headquarters with the news. The Lord was looking out for me that day. That was the third time I should've been killed. If my temperature had been one degree higher I would've been right beside my friends, as patients capable of doing so were allowed to place their cot wherever they wanted.

Every once in a while we'd get replacement troops, twenty-five to fifty at a time. I saw many different occupational specialties. For example, we had truck drivers who were forced to fight as infantry, because there were no trucks in the jungle. The new men were nervous, of course, and couldn't sleep when they heard explosions nearby. Perhaps it was unkind of us, but we veterans would throw the odd grenade during the night so the replacements would stay awake. That gave us someone alert and on guard, and provided us older men a chance to sleep. Of course, we were no older than the replacements, but we felt we had aged considerably by the experiences we'd endured in the last few weeks. We could only sleep if we knew someone was watching for movement. Incidentally, the bad thing about our grenades was that they left a few sparkles in a trail behind the grenade, so alert Japanese could see where they came from. The normal benefit of using grenades is that they didn't give away your position like a rifle muzzle flash would. Aussie grenades didn't have that problem, so we preferred to use them at night, though as mentioned earlier, they were no good when wet. The bottom line is that we could've used new grenades, and lots of them.

The Royal Australian Air Force had few resources, but what they did have they used with great bravery. For most of the battle for Buna's airfields, our battalion only had one artillery piece, and it was partially broken. That made the air forces that much more important. While it was hard for the faster US aircraft to spot the Japanese in the jungle, Australians in slower Wirraway trainers would fly low over enemy positions and daringly get the Japanese to shoot at them, revealing enemy positions. Though the Wirraways didn't carry bombs, sometimes the pilots would fly right over Japanese positions and drop grenades down at them, or would act as spotters for mortars or our one artillery piece.

Around Christmas time, possibly the day after Christmas, a close friend of mine in Company L, Private James Cross, a farm boy from Oklahoma, was severely wounded when an exploding shell hit him just below the knee.

The impact blew his leg clean off. He was probably hit by a round fired from an Anti-Aircraft Artillery (AAA) piece. Though designed to fire at aircraft, when cranked down and aimed horizontally, the AAA guns could be devastating against ground troops. I saw James being carried by natives back toward the rear. He made it through okay, and later settled in Ardmore, Oklahoma, in a specially-modified house provided by the VA.

I was never wounded in combat, at least nothing I was evacuated to the rear for. I'm not sure what the procedures for evacuating and processing our casualties were, except during an attack we marked the location of the wounded for medics by sticking a rifle with bayonet fixed in the ground next to the wounded. We couldn't stop to care for any men who went down. We were told to move on and keep fighting. The medics behind us would have to take care of them. Just about every squad had a medic. But more than twice as many men were out of action for fever as from battle wounds. New Guinea was a miserable place in which to fight.

In New Guinea I was often thankful to God. When you hear bullets sing by you, you know what it is; other men are trying their best to kill you, to end your life. You know you can be killed at any time. When the bullets were singing, I got close to the Lord. I stopped and prayed, though I think the prayers may have been a little heavy on requests for protection back then. I was just beginning to take my faith seriously, but I was growing. During the actual battle, too much was going on to think much about anything but staying alive and doing the job. Later, though, I thanked God for watching out for me. There was a long time in New Guinea when I didn't think I would make it back. At one point, we attacked every morning, and when I saw someone go down next to me I thought, "Well, I guess I'm next." I knew I was going to get it any day. I thought each attack would be my last. Many times I thought, "These are my last moments on earth." I saw good men go down all around me. Then we'd get the upper hand, or the fighting would taper off, and maybe the Lord gave me a little bit extra pep to get through it. When I made it through a battle, I'd think, "Well, we made it through again, Lord." I think all the men considered they'd die. I didn't over-analyze it, though. I knew that in many places in the New Testament it says that if anyone believes that Jesus is God's Son, confesses Him as Lord, and is baptized into Him, he/she will have eternal life. I had made peace with God, and I was ready to die. That was it.

During the war, I often attended church services, and I sat on many a log in the front lines, when we did have services. Of course, we didn't have services very often when we were fighting. It was up to each man to gain his peace with God. Before we went into combat, chaplains gave each of us a pocket New Testament, but after living in the mud and the swamps and the rain, it was no good. It was soaked. I think they should've given us another one later on. At that point I wished I had memorized more scripture passages, so that I could bring them to mind when I had time to think, there on the front lines, lying in the rain, or hunkered down behind a tree. For the first time in my life, when I really wanted one, I had no Bible, no New Testament. We had a battalion chaplain, but the chaplains would rotate in every so often. I can't remember any of their names, but I think on the whole they did a good job.

During those days of battle, a lot of men thought about spiritual things. When the bullets started coming close, most of us thought about death. I didn't have any deep spiritual discussions during our months in combat, but I did later. I think everybody was worried about getting killed. The men knew I was a Christian, and later, back in Australia, some of the men spoke to me about spiritual things.

Left to Right: Ty, Albert, and Robert Freese, Oklahoma City, early 1920s.

Robert Freese (far right) in the late 1920's with his family, Oklahoma City.

*Twenty-year-old Robert Freese trying out for the
Oklahoma City Indians baseball team, 1937.*

Native village near Wanigela, New Guinea.

Native chief near Wanigela, New Guinea.

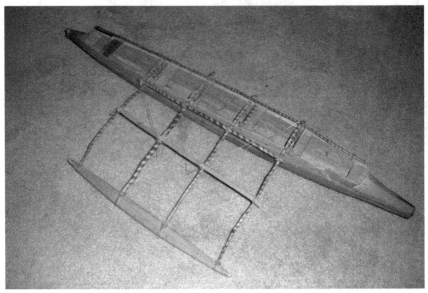

*Model made by natives of New Guinea - dugout canoe like the one
that ferried Company-L across the river in October 1942.*

Japanese landing craft destroyed near Cape Endaiadere (Maggot Beach), New Guinea, 1942.

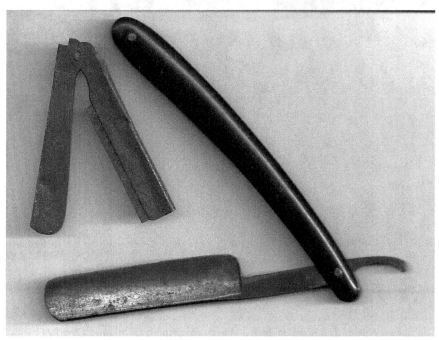

Japanese razors Robert Freese found in a bunker during the Battle of Buna. Enlisted man's razor (L), and officer's (R), December 1942.

Leona Nievar as a nurse trainee at Mercy Hospital in Oklahoma City, 1943.

Robert Freese at the Dobadura jungle training camp, New Guinea.

--⊰ **DOMAIN OF THE GOLDEN DRAGON** ⊱--
TO ALL SAILORS, SOLDIERS, AND MARINES
**WHEREVER YE MAY BE AND TO ALL MERMAIDS, FLYING DRAGONS,
SPIRITS OF THE DEEP, DEVIL CHASERS**
--⊰ **GREETINGS** ⊱--

KNOW YE that on this **25** day of **Sept.**, 19 **44**,
in latitude............ longitude............ there appeared within my
august dwelling the........ **"Sea CaT"**

HEARKEN YE: That said vessel, officers and crew have been inspected
and passed on by my august body and staff. And know ye:
that ....**Sgt. Maurice R. Freese**............
having been found sane and worthy to be numbered a dweller of the
FAR EAST has been gathered in my fold and duly initiated into the

SILENT MYSTERIES OF THE FAR EAST

BE IT FURTHER UNDERSTOOD: That by virtue of the power vested in
me I do hereby command all moneylenders, wine sellers, cabaret owners,
cat house managers and all my other subjects to show honor and respect
to all his wishes whenever he may enter my realm.
· **Disobey this command under penalty of my august displeasure.**

By his servant....**Arrow McLean** **GOLDEN DRAGON**
Chieftain Ruler of the 180th Meridian

*On 25 September, 1944, Robert Freese had two 28th birthdays when he
crossed the International Dateline in the Sea Cat hospital ship.*

Sergeant Maurice Robert Freese, US Army, 1944.

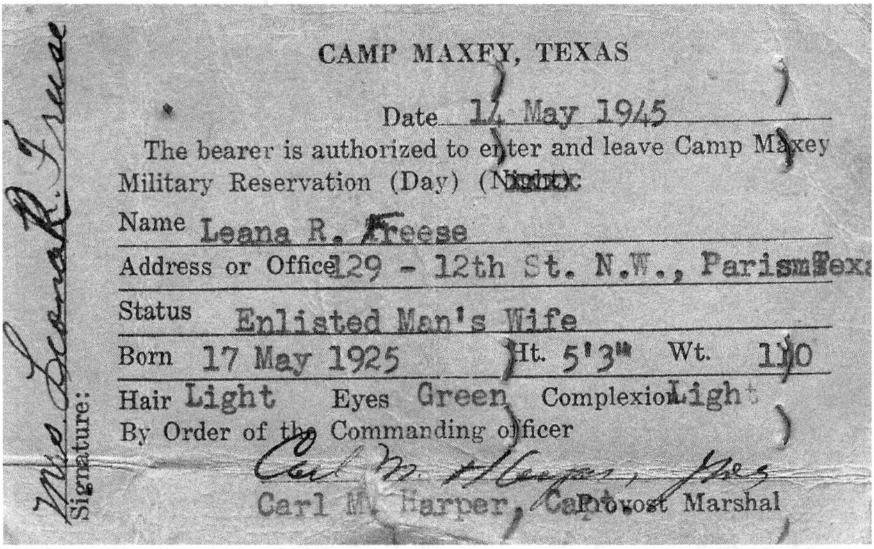

CAMP MAXEY, TEXAS

Date 14 May 1945

The bearer is authorized to enter and leave Camp Maxey Military Reservation (Day) (Night)

Name Leana R. Freese

Address or Office 129 - 12th St. N.W., Paris, Texa

Status Enlisted Man's Wife

Born 17 May 1925 Ht. 5'3" Wt. 110

Hair Light Eyes Green Complexion Light

By Order of the Commanding officer

Carl M. Harper, Capt.

Carl M. Harper, Capt. Provost Marshal

Signature: Mrs Leona R. Freese

Leona Freese's Camp Maxey base pass, 1945.

Robert and Leona Freese in January 1946, less than four months after Robert was discharged from the Army.

Robert Freese in 1951.

Robert and Leona in the early 1950's.

Leona holds newborn David, with Trish (top), and Jean - February 1955

*Robert and Leona Freese in 1987 with their grown
children David Freese and Trish Carnes.*

*Robert and Leona Freese at their 50th Anniversary celebration,
November 1994, Draper Park Christian Church.*

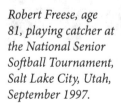

*Robert Freese, age
81, playing catcher at
the National Senior
Softball Tournament,
Salt Lake City, Utah,
September 1997.*

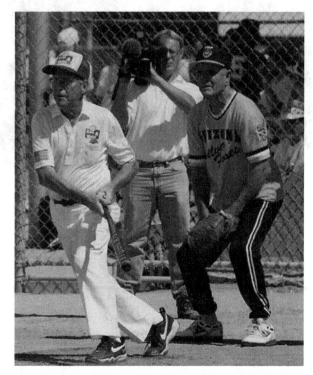

Robert and Leona Freese in September 2009.

CHAPTER SIX:
DRIVING THE ENEMY OUT

One day, on the coast near Cape Endaiadere, we saw waves of Japanese fighters and bombers approaching from over the ocean, apparently from the big Japanese base at Rabaul in New Britain. As I recall, there were about fifty aircraft in the attack. We were dug in at the beach at the time, in slit trenches, less than 200 feet from the water. We were supposed to be farther inland, with the Australians on the coast to our right. However, due to swamp and thick jungle conditions inland, we were bunched up right on the coast with the Australians, a good target for Japanese aircraft. When we heard the incoming aircraft, we knew they weren't ours. Ours had a smoother sound; theirs sounded like washing machines. We looked up when we heard the washing machine sound. They were about medium height. It was clear they were out to bomb us, and we were all pretty scared, awaiting our destruction, and not being able to do anything about it. We were sitting ducks. But then something amazing happened. Four brave US pilots in twin-engine, twin-tailed P-38 Lightnings brazenly flew at the Japanese formation, guns blazing. It was all very near, over our heads and out over the ocean next to us. To our delight, the sudden attack by our fighters disrupted the enemy bombing run, causing the bombers to release their ordnance early. Most of the bombs fell short, into the water. When the bombs hit the water, water filled our trenches—that's how close to the coast we were. I watched four Japanese aircraft go down, all blasted from the sky by a single P-38 as he made a wide circle in the distance. Then, trailing smoke, he lost altitude and dropped low over the water. The pilot obviously didn't want to go down over the ocean. He skimmed in right in front of my position and crash-landed on the beach, less than a hundred yards in front of me.

US Army Air Forces P-38 Lightning.

Every morning, something like 0700, we charged the Japanese positions. You could set your clock by it. So it seemed natural that when the American P-38 went down right in front of us, my company, accompanied by an Australian unit, attacked the Japanese positions in front of us to our north in order to save the pilot. The Japanese began shooting at us and the pilot simultaneously. Bullets were flying in all directions. By the time we fought our way to the downed fighter, the pilot was already out of the cockpit. The Australians were pinned down by heavy Japanese machine gun and rifle fire and didn't make it to the plane, but Company L did.

The pilot was wounded; he could barely walk. Once we had him safely in our care, we fell back 100 yards to our original positions, as the crash site was dangerously close to enemy pillboxes. Later we would find that there wasn't a single row of pillboxes, but three rows. I thought it was quite an achievement to save the pilot right under the noses of the Japanese. Two or three men took the pilot back to battalion headquarters, which was only a hundred yards behind us. In the thick jungle, everything was closer than in open warfare, but much harder to get to. Later, when the navy boys came in with supplies, they took the pilot back to the rear with them. I didn't see the other three American pilots, but I understand they all went down. Two pilots had to bail out and one nursed his fighter back to an American airbase and crash-landed. All our pilots survived. It was an exciting and successful day. The Army Air Forces boys saved us, then we saved one of them. We lost some men in saving that pilot, but then we lost men in every attack. Later that day or the next, Tokyo Rose, which the Japanese broadcast with loudspeakers fixed to coconut trees on their side of the front line, said they shot down Richard Bong. He would later become the most famous, top scoring US ace of World War II, with forty kills. I don't know if it was really him we saved or not, but I know Richard Bong did fly out of Port Moresby, and certainly flew combat sorties in our area when I was there. Of course, I wouldn't know Major Bong if I saw him. Incidentally, Tokyo Rose often told us when we were going to be attacked, and it usually happened as she said it would.

Japanese forces tried to reinforce their men in the Buna area with new men and equipment, using PT-type boats and barges, and even airdropping small quantities of supplies using Zero fighters. As late as December, the Japanese were able to land hundreds of additional troops, but our fighters caught their barges and landing craft in the open and sank some of them, then came back the next morning and strafed the supplies they had just unloaded on the beach. The Japanese thereafter found they couldn't resupply their men in the Buna area, due to the actions of our air force. At that point, without resupply, the Japanese troops knew they only had two choices—retreat up the coast to the north, or die in place fighting for the emperor. Unfortunately for Japanese troops squeezed against the coast near Cape Endaidere, we had cut off their escape route to the north. Their situation was desperate, and the only logical thing for their commander to do was surrender and save the lives of his men. But still they refused to surrender, no matter how untenable their position. The Japanese gave us no choice but to kill every last one of them, or be killed ourselves.

The Japanese became more desperate and began to conduct counterattacks. They fixed bayonets and screamed something awful before they attacked. I saw a lot of American soldiers go down, some of them close friends of mine.

I witnessed buddies being bayoneted or machine gunned. It was brutal; the enemy knew the Imperial Japanese Navy wouldn't be able to rescue them. The AAF took care of that. US fighters patrolled the sea between the New Guinea coast and the big Japanese naval airbase at Rabaul to the northeast.

As we fought our way north, we had to enter Japanese bunkers to clear them one-by-one, normally after an intense firefight. We had about a dozen M3 Stuart light tanks with us by this time, operating mainly along the shoreline, though in places engineers felled trees and made primitive roads for the tanks through the swamps. We got into 90% of the bunkers by using tanks in the following manner. A Stuart tank would move forward and fire its relatively small 37mm main gun at a bunker. It would take two or three of these shells to penetrate the robust walls. Eventually the shells would blast through, and that would stun the defenders inside. Then an infantryman would have to go in. It seemed the task fell to me a disproportionate number of times, though I'm sure others thought the same about themselves. It was often semi-dark in the Japanese positions. I would've given anything for a pistol, but I wasn't issued one—they just weren't available. We didn't have many grenades either (it seemed we were always short of what we really needed); we had to go in with bayonets. I took my bayonet off my rifle and used it as a knife many times. Sometimes, I would enter a bunker to find the enemy blown to pieces or with gunshot or shrapnel wounds. Often, wounded or stunned Japanese would roll on their stomachs while clutching a grenade, hoping that when I rolled them over the grenade would kill us both. I was afraid to bayonet an enemy soldier as soon as I came upon him because that might move his body and set off a live grenade with the pin pulled. So I learned to reach one hand under the enemy's stomach to feel for a grenade, while clutching my bayonet in the other. If there was a live grenade, I would grab it, spin around, and toss it out of the bunker, and hope it didn't hit someone, or hit something and bounce back at me. All this while somehow trying to kill the guy who just tried to kill us both. The other members of my squad would stay away from the bunker until I called out that it was safe. Crawling into these pillboxes was the worst job I ever had. Sometimes, when others had the job, my buddies would crawl into a bunker and not crawl out.

When I had to go into a pillbox alone, I really thought I wouldn't make it out. The best place to enter a pillbox was from the rear, where there might be an entrance, or where it was often more open, but even the back of a pillbox was covered in logs, dirt, fifty-five gallon barrels filled with earth, and all of it covered in vegetation. Of course, there could be an active enemy pillbox behind the one we were attacking, too, with enemy soldiers firing at us. If the entrance was tall and in a more open area, I could use my rifle with bayonet attached, but more often than not, I had to remove the bayonet and crawl into the entrance on my belly. Whoever was closest to the entrance would normally go in first, or sometimes, whoever was in charge would try to be fair and we'd take turns. Sometimes the lowest-ranking man had to go. In any case, it seemed to be my turn a lot. It was in these circumstances that I wished, if I didn't have a pistol, at least I could have a knife. The bayonet was too long for this close-in work.

One time, a soldier from our platoon crawled into a pillbox where we thought all the enemy soldiers had been killed. After a few minutes without his return we knew tragedy had befallen him. He was probably clubbed or bayoneted to death, because we didn't hear any rifle fire or explosions. Someone else would have to go in. One of my buddies then crawled in the back of the pillbox on his belly, bayonet in hand, with me right behind him. Inside we found four Japanese soldiers stunned or wounded, but ready to fight to the death. We killed them all. I don't know if I killed any of the Japanese soldiers I was shooting at with my rifle or the machine gun during the Battle of Buna, but I killed a lot of men up close with my bayonet.

Fighting the Japanese was so brutal because they knew if they pursued the war in a conventional way, within the limits of conventional military norms, they'd be defeated by the much larger United States with our vast natural resources. So Japan's leaders determined that they'd extract such a ghastly blood price for every US gain, that this "nation of storekeepers," as they called us, would be driven to negotiations rather than accept the cost in human lives. They also had an arrogance that came with a belief in the superiority of the Japanese soldier and his fighting spirit, even though many of their weapons were inferior to ours. Like many living in a closed society (like the Nazis), they believed their own propaganda. The average Japanese soldier, until the New Guinea campaign, believed he would never retreat, could never be beaten. Since invading Manchuria in 1931, he never had. The Japanese soldier displayed a courage and capacity for suffering that was hard to believe, and terrified us. From basic training onward, Japanese soldiers were subjected to conditioning more brutal even than that of the Russians. But they greatly misjudged the abilities and fighting spirit of the American soldier, sailor, and airman, and how hard a free man will fight for his country.[1]

I only saw one Japanese prisoner taken, and I learned, to my surprise, that he'd attended the University of New York. I've read that there were other prisoners taken in the campaign, but I never saw any. I didn't speak to the one I did see, but I was close enough to see he had a head wound, which had been bandaged by our medics. Natives were dispatched to take him to the rear, a hike of about ten miles. Four natives left with him, but returned ten minutes later, minus their prisoner. When I saw the natives were back already I knew they had finished him off.

Right during the battle for Buna, sometime in mid-December, we were given some Australian hardtack (rock-hard bread) that was so tough I broke one of my upper left teeth on it. It hurt so badly that I received permission to make my way back to the battalion aid station. Once I got there, to my dismay the medics could offer nothing for the pain. One medic held me down while a medic we called "Rosie" (I don't know why) sawed around the tooth with a scalpel to cut the skin on the gums loose, in the process removing a lot of flesh unnecessarily. Then he grabbed the tooth with some sort of pliers and started working it. He pulled on it, and worked it back and forth, for what seemed an eternity, and finally yanked it out, holding it up triumphantly. I bled like a stuck hog. I'm sure "Rosie" had no training whatsoever in pulling teeth, but normally he doctored the men as best he could. He gave me a tablet to swallow. I don't know what it was, but it certainly didn't help the pain.

Sometime after this, as we were still trying to reach the Buna airfields, some meager supplies in the form of cans of peaches arrived. I ate one-third of a peach and passed the can on to the next man. That's how precious a can of peaches was—the can would have to be shared among many. I watched my company commander, Captain Sammy Horton, give his share to another man, though we were all practically starving at the time. That's true leadership.

The day after we got the meager ration of peaches, six new M3 Stuart light tanks arrived. They were soon lost in a furious fight with three Japanese pill-boxes at the corner of the southern-most (New) airstrip. Unfortunately, the middle bunker held the three-inch naval gun the enemy used as a direct-fire weapon. It fired at almost point-blank range at the tanks, blowing them up one by one. However, I believe the naval gun was also destroyed in the battle. We had to wait a couple weeks for more tanks, since by now our leadership began to fully grasp that charging the bunkers without tanks was foolish and a needless waste of lives.

94

米軍は俘虜を優遇する。俘虜の待遇に關する國際條約の締約國として、米國は字義通りそれを遵奉し、その待遇は米國兵士に對するものと殆んど變らない。以下同條約文を引用すれば

第二條（俘虜ハ）如何ナル場合ニモ情義ヲ以テ待遇サルベク特ニ暴力行爲、嘲罵、或ハ公衆ノ好奇心ヨリ保護サルベシ

第十條─俘虜ハ、衛生上保健ニ出來得ル限リ留意セル建物又ハ營舍ニ收容サルベシ

第十一條─俘虜ノ糧食ハ、ソノ量質共ニ（拘留軍基地ニ於ケル）兵士ノ糧食ト同等ナルベシ……喫煙ハ許サル

米軍の俘虜は米軍兵士と同等の食事を支給されるから、下表に見る通り日本でいへば東京で一流の帝國ホテル邊りで食べられるものを毎日與へられる。以下、米軍兵士毎日の糧食を示すと

魚及び肉類　　　一三六匁
米及びパン　　　九五匁
馬鈴薯　　　　　七五匁
野菜類　　　　　八四匁
穀類　　　　　　一匁三分
果實類　　　　　三五匁二分
砂糖　　　　　　三七匁七分
牛乳　　　　　　六八匁
バタ、其他脂肪類二四匁八分
茶、コーヒー　　一七匁八分

Security Pass

TO ALL MEMBERS OF THE UNITED STATES ARMED FORCES:

The bearer of this pass is su...e is to be treated courteously and escorted to the nearest commanding officer, who will arrange for his transfer out of the combat area. He probably understands no English but has been instructed to obey sign orders.

Commanding Officer of the United States Forces
（日本文ハ裏面ニアリ）

A Surrender leaflet dropped by the Army Air Forces at Buna that Robert brought home with him.

95

On the 21st of December, Allied aircraft dropped leaflets on the enemy emplacements that read "SOLDIERS OF THE JAPANESE ARMY: Our Allied Forces are steadily advancing on all fronts...You are already doomed. Your situation is hopeless."[2] I'm not aware of a single Japanese soldier surrendering because of them. What really mattered was resupply and heavy weapons. As we received more mortars and artillery, in addition to the vital tanks and replacement troops, the Japanese bunkers finally became truly vulnerable. We captured the southern airfield, only after receiving twenty-five to thirty new replacements and some new tanks. We took the main airfield (Old Strip) on about December 28, by walking behind the newly-arrived tanks as they moved right down the airstrip, from the southeast to the northwest, after we had painstakingly cleared all the bunkers, one at a time, using the tank's firepower combined with infantry.

On the southeastern corner of the last airfield (Old Strip) Private Philip Dorn and I came across a bunker-like cellar, different from the pillboxes we'd seen. We cautiously entered the darkened room, and saw it contained no enemy soldiers, but quite a few bags of rice, plus canned fish, with the tails and heads still attached. There was also quite a supply of Imperial Marine uniforms. We selected some uniforms with which to clothe ourselves, and then, as we had not eaten in four or five days, sat on the bags and ate all the rice we wanted. We opened cans of fish with our bayonets. I couldn't eat the fish heads with those big, staring, eyeballs, so I bit off the tail ends and threw away the heads. Before long, a lieutenant entered the cellar and said, "Hey, what are you doing, eating that Jap food? Don't you know they could've poisoned it?" I suppose they could've, but it didn't do either one of us any harm, and we were hungry enough to take a chance. The lieutenant then noticed we were wearing enemy uniforms, and ordered us to take them off. He was afraid someone would mistake us for the enemy and shoot us. Interestingly, Imperial Marines were often chosen for their size, and that may be the only reason I found a uniform that fit my 5' 11" frame. My Army-issued fatigues were literally rotting off my body. I'd already cut my trousers to shorts. My shoes were so rotten that the sole had come apart and started flapping when I walked, so I had to cut the sole out. I was barefoot at the front of my shoes, and my feet had jungle rot. The Japanese uniforms were new and of good quality. I hated to take my new attire off, but then I didn't want to be shot by mistake either.

By January 2, 1943, we had the Japanese pushed off the Old Airstrip and then north right to the coast. We pushed in closer with our attack, yard by yard toward the beach. When the moment came that they knew they'd be wiped out for certain, the Japanese troops waded into the ocean and tried to make it across the bay to the Cape, swimming or clinging to anything they could. We fought our way to the beach and watched the remnants attempt their escape. As they swam away we shot them down, like ducks in the water. Both American and Australian soldiers were banging away at the enemy, now finally out in the open where we could see them. We waited until we could see their heads bobbing up above the waves, and then fired. Artillery opened up on them. The AAF flew over later in the morning and strafed those still in the water. After so painfully trying to root them out of hardened, dug-in positions, it was almost sheer joy to see our enemies out in the open. For once, they were the ones vulnerable. I don't think there was a single man among the filthy, bearded, exhausted, and traumatized veterans who was sorry to finally see the destruction of our enemy in large numbers. Virtually every one of the Japanese defenders in that area was killed. When the tide came in, it washed scores of enemy bodies ashore; in some places at the water's edge, bodies were five or six deep. With the heat an intense 125 degrees, the bodies began rotting in a day. Everyone began to call Cape Endaiadere "Maggot Beach," and the name stuck. This area of New Guinea's coast would be forever known as "Maggot Beach." Later I saw the February 15, 1943, Life magazine photo spread of Maggot Beach, through which the Battle of Buna became well known.

On Maggot Beach, ten of us had one gallon of bully beef (in this case not really beef but Australian mutton) to share between us. Despite being half-starved, none of the other nine men would touch it. So, I sat down on the beach and ate most of the gallon myself. I was hungry despite the bodies all around us covered with maggots, and the wretched taste of the meat itself. I didn't let the scene around me or the smell stop me. I had gone hungry a long time.

The capture of the Old Airfield and Maggot Beach ended the Battle for Buna, but small groups of Japanese troops who had escaped were all around us. It would be some time before all enemy stragglers were mopped up. On January 22, 1943, the Buna-Gona-Sanananda campaign officially ended. For the first time in the war, the Allies had defeated the Japanese in a land battle.

Together with the US Marine Corps victory at Guadalcanal two weeks later, it gave the American public hope that we could indeed beat the Japanese, on land, sea, or in the air.

After we took Buna, we remained in the area until about the middle of February, while the 127th Regiment and the 41st Infantry Division continued the fight on up the coast with the battle for Lae. However, our regiment had been decimated, our company (normally about 160 men) reduced to ten men, and for us the battle was over, our objectives finally won. The 128th Infantry Regiment was right in the middle of the Battle of Buna, and paid a dear price. When we started out I was in the third platoon, L-Company. But later there were so many casualties that we were just L-Company. There weren't any platoons. At Buna, L-Company was nearly wiped out multiple times as a fighting unit. Most men were emaciated and ill, and we lost others to wounds or death. Our numbers continually decreased. Yet we had the jungle experience needed, and more than the experience, each survivor was one more man needed so desperately. Somehow the company survived as a unit as replacements were brought in to add to the very few of us left.

We walked back to Dobodura to be airlifted to Port Moresby, but had to wait about a week until the weather was right to fly over the imposing Owen Stanley Range. We settled in and built shelters and cots using nothing but the raw materials provided by the jungle. Still, this was the first time since we left Australia that we were able to make any kind of decent shelter to ward off the heavy rain. By the end of January, it no longer rained the three or four times a day we were used to, keeping us wet and miserable most of the time, but we experienced the even worse constant monsoon rains.

Finally we flew back to Port Moresby, and the first thing we did was eat. What I remember about this meal prepared for returning warriors fresh from battle is that little black bugs speckled the bread. Maybe that's not what we'd been dreaming about for our first meal in the rear area, but we ate it all. I don't remember getting sick from the unaccustomed experience of a full stomach; we were already sick with too many other things and it didn't really make any difference. We were then issued new uniforms and weighed. When they weighed me I found I was 148 pounds, down from the 196 pounds I weighed when we left Australia five months before. Thanks to the hard training required for the baseball team, I had been in great shape. After the battle of Buna, I was a shell of my former self.

We were tired, dirty, and hungry. One man described it like this: "The men at the front in New Guinea were perhaps the most wretched-looking soldiers ever to wear the American uniform. They were gaunt and thin, with deep black circles under their sunken eyes. They were covered with tropical sores…They were clothed in tattered, stained shirts and pants…often the soles had been sucked off their shoes by the tenacious, stinking mud. Many of them fought for days with fevers…malaria, dengue fever, dysentery, and in a few cases, typhus hit man after man. There was hardly a soldier, among the thousands who went into the jungle, who didn't come down with some kind of fever at least once."[3]

Only three men from the Division baseball team were accounted for after the battle—a young soldier from Arizona, Bob Teeples, and myself--only the three of us. Later, in Australia again, we would largely need to build a whole new team.

CHAPTER SEVEN:
BACK IN AUSTRALIA

From Port Moresby on New Guinea's southeastern coast, we sailed to Brisbane in mid-February 1943, and upon arrival climbed into trucks for the thirty-mile trip south to Camp Cable. The ride through Brisbane was refreshing, as we absorbed the sights and sounds of a modern western city again, or at least what I could see looking past several other men through the canvas opening at the back of the truck. After the misery of five months in the jungle, it was a most welcome sight. I think most of us never expected to see Brisbane again. Forty minutes later we pulled off the highway and turned left toward Camp Cable. We crossed the railroad tracks a half mile from the highway and were waved through the main gate by the military police. We were home. I looked forward to the familiarity of Camp Cable, the relative luxury of sleeping on a cot in a tent, and enjoying three square meals a day.

At Camp Cable we received replacement troops, and immediately went to work training them. Company L received about a hundred and fifty replacements, including officers and NCOs. All L-Company's original platoon leaders, who were normally lieutenants, had been killed or wounded, as had a number of their replacements. My platoon didn't get a replacement officer until at least a month after we returned to Brisbane. We were down to two sergeants for the entire company, so I was temporarily made a platoon sergeant. Without an officer present, I led the platoon. Most of the training I provided the new troops was conducted at Camp Cable, which, being thirty miles outside Brisbane, was really out in the country, with plenty of land surrounding our camp on which to train. I ensured the platoon became proficient at field stripping weapons, tossing grenades, and bayoneting. I also taught them what trees in New Guinea held the most water, and what berries they should and should not eat.

Captain Horton was very ill when we returned to Australia. Being older than most of us, in his late 30's or early 40's, his legs were more adversely affected than others by all the days spent in New Guinea swamps, and he could no longer walk. He was soon admitted to the hospital, and, shortly after Captain Horton left, my malaria began acting up again, and I left for the hospital myself. I had trained the new troops for just two weeks before leaving for three weeks of malaria treatment. I'd be in and out of hospitals such that two of the six months back in Australia after the Battle of Buna were spent convalescing from malaria.

In Australia, I also had trouble sleeping and began to experience nightmares, which were to continue for years after the war. About once a week I'd have a vivid dream involving a friend being killed before my eyes, though the man in my dream had no specific identity. I also had nightmares about Japanese soldiers I'd killed, and worried about what God thought of me taking the lives of others. I preferred my days to be busy so my thoughts would be on something else. Training the replacement soldiers kept my mind off the Battle of Buna and gave me purpose, as I knew the training would help the new soldiers stay alive in the next battle. I felt sorry for the replacements, knowing what was in store for them. Rumors were flying that the 32nd Infantry Division would be back in action before long, just as soon as we could get the division up to something resembling normal strength. I was also glad to be playing baseball, as it was an effective way to keep my mind off the horrors of New Guinea.

After a few months back in Australia, dining at the officers' mess (with their better food), and rigorously conditioning with the baseball team, I was able to regain my health to a large extent, as well as my weight. By now I had made it back to about 190 pounds. The new division ball team, composed almost entirely of new players, did quite well. In fact, we ended up winning the Australian championship in 1943. When I wasn't training the replacement troops, I was playing ball. I was happy to immerse myself in the game for a while, and try to forget what I'd seen and done.

Sometime after I returned to Australia, Leona Nievar sent me her photo. I hadn't thought much about courtship or marriage, because to be honest, I didn't think I'd be coming home. I figured I was going to "get it" one of these days. But now that there was some hope, I began to write to her again, and I kept her photo throughout my tour overseas. It was a tremendous boost to my morale to get letters from her.

One day, I had the platoon spread out in rows on a training field to clean their weapons. Some of the men had Tommy Guns, and some had bolt-action M1903s like mine, but most had M1 Garands. Months earlier I'd given the M1903 that had seen me through the battle after my M1 was shot out of my hands a cursory cleaning. However, I hadn't had a chance to clean it thoroughly since the Battle of Buna. I thought this would be a good time to do it, while I gave the members of my platoon some practical advice on what the jungle can do to their weapons. As I removed the pieces, I carefully laid them on an army-green towel on the ground in front of me, one-by-one in order, so the parts would be easier to reassemble. A fresh first lieutenant replacement, scheduled to replace Captain Horton as our new company commander, approached me. Without so much as a "Hello Sergeant, how are things going here?," he began mouthing off, saying, "Look here, Sergeant. You should know Field Manual 23-10 expressly forbids removal of the trigger guard for cleaning. Just whadda ya think you're doing?!" I was amazed he'd chastise me in front of my men. His display was unprofessional and undermined my authority. As to the subject at hand, my M1903 was abnormally dirty after being abused for so long in the jungle, so I had to break it down completely to clean it properly. After he chewed me out, he kicked the pieces onto the dirt, scattering all the little parts. I knew how Field Manual 23-10 read, but the men who wrote the field manual had never fought in the jungle. The lieutenant had never been in any kind of battle and knew nothing about combat or what we'd been through in New Guinea. I'd just returned from some of the most wretched fighting American soldiers anywhere had experienced. I'd been conditioned to kill, and I had killed many. Now this young lieutenant was berating me in front of my men, regarding a subject he knew nothing about. I guess the lieutenant touched a nerve.

Without saying a word, I stood up and busted the lieutenant in the mouth, laying him out on the ground. He was stunned for a moment, then looked up at me, glaring, and picked himself off the ground. He dusted himself off, and retreated toward battalion headquarters. I can't say I was thinking anything then, except, "Well, I guess I'm going to the jug."

That same evening, there was a court martial. Two of the 128th Regiment's leaders, Lieutenant Colonel Alexander McNabb (128th Infantry Regiment's Executive Officer) and Lieutenant Colonel Kelsie Miller (my 3rd Battalion Commander) sat on my court martial. Within a few minutes I went from sergeant to private. I was also given a sentence of confinement, though I can't remember how long it was supposed to be. I think they had mercy on me, because the punishment for assaulting an officer could've been more severe. The two officers presiding at my court martial attended all the ball games, and both of them were Okies like me. Lieutenant Colonel Miller was from the Oklahoma City area, and Lieutenant Colonel McNabb had been an ROTC instructor at Oklahoma State before the war. I had "Okie" written on my hat. Both men had also observed my performance in battle. The lieutenant, who foolishly chastised a combat veteran for how thoroughly he was cleaning his rifle, was probably not looked on too favorably. We never saw him again.

My new home, the stockade, was a group of tents surrounded by a twenty foot high fence. To my surprise, as a member of the division baseball team I was still expected to go into Brisbane and play baseball on behalf of the division, even though I was a prisoner. Initially, the rest of the team left in trucks the next day, while I sat in jail. A short time later, however, the lieutenant in charge of the ball team came by, intending to have me released so I could catch up with them. A stand-off ensued. The lieutenant in charge of the stockade wouldn't let me go; I was his prisoner. Next, Lieutenant Colonel Miller and Lieutenant Colonel McNabb came after me, but the stockade lieutenant refused again. Finally, a general came, quickly gained my release, and took me into Brisbane in the front of his staff car. After playing that weekend, I was dropped off at the stockade for the night. Each weekday morning I was to return to the company to train troops, and each afternoon I left to play ball. In what was probably not the most brilliant move for a prisoner, I refused to train corporals and sergeants because, thanks to the court martial,

I was now a private. I didn't think I should train troops who outranked me, as I now lacked authority. I just refused. I guess I may have had a stubborn streak. I don't know how I got by with it. I can't say how many men were at the stockade, or really much about it at all. I just spent nights there, and Monday through Thursday nights at that. I don't know how long I was supposed to be incarcerated, because after just nineteen days in the stockade, I was released to return to combat.

CHAPTER EIGHT: AMPHIBIOUS ASSAULTS

Sometime about August 1943, two companies from 3rd Battalion were selected to conduct amphibious operations on a couple of small islands. We
were driven to Brisbane harbour (as the Aussies spell it) and loaded into a
big coal-burning ship. We left Brisbane and sailed north about 1,200 miles,
then northeast around the southeastern-most "tail" of New Guinea. While
aboard ship we were told we'd be landing on Goodenough Island, not far
off the coast from where we'd fought almost a year before. An airfield oc-
cupied the southern end of the island, and it was important that we keep it
out of Japanese hands. There were also a number of Japanese soldiers and
sailors on the island. They were either coast watchers who reported Allied
ship movements, or survivors of downed aircraft or ships sunk as a result of
Allied action. They may have also been remnants of the task forces that had
attacked Milne Bay or been ejected from the Buna area. In any case there
had been a lot of air and sea activity between the battles of Guadalcanal and
Buna, and I wasn't surprised to know that some Japanese elements had been
scattered throughout the island chains known as the D'Entrecasteaux and the
Trobriand Islands.

Years later I would discover that the information we'd been given aboard ship was wrong. The one by seven mile island that we landed on couldn't possibly have been Goodenough Island, which was fifteen by twenty miles, and at the time had an Australian airfield. The Australians landed on Goodenough back in October 1942, while I was thrashing around the jungle, interestingly, near Goodenough Bay, from which Goodenough Island was visible.

This episode just highlights the confusion with which all soldiers must contend. Our job was to do what we were told, and for the most part the common GIs were dependent on information from their leadership. We knew very little of what was going on outside our immediate perspective. To this day I don't know the name of the island, or if it even had a name. All I know for certain is, we weren't in Oklahoma.

Our ship slowed to a crawl and then dropped anchor near the island—a mile or two from the beach we climbed down a web of ropes hung over the side of the ship and transferred to landing craft. We hit the beach with no Japanese opposition. L-Company's job was to secure the beach, then the airfield, while the other company came in behind us and climbed the single mountain on the island, looking for Japanese stragglers who escaped into the higher elevations. The overall mission was to clear the island of Japanese so a signal unit could set up some sort of communication station.

The island was only a mile across, but ran north and south for seven miles. We landed on the western side of the island and secured the beach. I saw no Japanese troops at all the first day.

The next day I was promoted to sergeant again. Since we'd regrouped in Australia, most of 3rd Battalion's men were replacements, and experienced veterans were in demand. Our platoon pushed east across the island to link up with another platoon that had landed on the eastern side of the island. After we'd nearly worked our way across to the eastern side of the island, we spotted a squad of Japanese soldiers moving north toward the mountain, thankfully before they saw us. They were still a few hundred yards away. The island wasn't as thickly forested as New Guinea, and we couldn't slip in as close to them as we would've liked, but at least it was a lot easier to move around. We were able to get a little closer to them, but were eventually spotted. When the enemy soldiers noticed us closing behind them, they fired in our direction and most of us began shooting at them. The gunfight lasted a few minutes, until our foes withdrew up the mountain into the jungle. None of our men were hit. When we arrived at the point where the Japanese had been, we found nothing. Either we missed them altogether or they pulled their dead and wounded out with them.

We turned our attention toward the southern end of the island. One of our squads had already turned south and was some distance ahead of us. They apparently pushed a number of Japanese toward the tip of the island, because we heard gunfire for a while, and then suddenly it stopped. At first we couldn't see anything. Once we'd caught up with them the other squad told us that they'd seen several Japanese troops, and had fired on them, but they'd disappeared. They weren't sure if they hit any of them or not.

We soon secured the airstrip, walking its full length. Of course on foot it seemed huge; I would've estimated that it was two miles long. The only aircraft at the airfield were a couple of derelict Japanese Zeros, which had either been shot up by Allied air forces while they sat on the ground, or crash landed on the island.

While the rest of the battalion went up behind us toward the mountain, L-Company carefully checked for stragglers around the airfield. When the area was considered safe, the signal corps landed and took over. L-Company was on the island only two or three days, though the others in the landing craft behind us who had to search the mountain (where we knew there were at least some Japanese—the ones we had flushed up there), stayed longer.

Leaving the island, we waded into the surf and boarded landing craft that shuttled us out to the ship. Later, after the rest of the force was brought back, we weighed anchor and sailed away, leaving the island behind.

After sailing for a day or two we made another landing, this time on Robinson Island. It was a small island, as far as I know of no particular significance. I'm not sure why we landed, because I never saw any Japanese there. Others may have. We were only there a day or two when we were ordered to return to the ship. From Robinson Island we sailed back to Brisbane.

At Camp Cable we were once again told to train incoming replacements, but some of us Buna veterans were sent to the hospital for malaria. I was sent to three hospitals after the amphibious operations. The standard treatment for malaria was to receive eighteen days of quinine treatment, but it rarely worked that way. I think the problem was the Army's supply of quinine. The hospital staff would try atabrine, which I knew from experience didn't work, and I'd be back within a few days with a high fever. They'd load me in an Army ambulance or 2 ½ ton truck with three or four others, and we'd be off to yet another hospital, perhaps one with a supply of quinine. I don't know why I was shuttled to so many different hospitals while I was overseas. It could well be based on the supplies each had on hand, or the hospital beds available. Maybe at times it was based on which were best at caring for malaria, given the level of symptoms.

A few weeks after we returned to Australia the second time, I went AWOL with James, one of the other nine men from L-Company who'd returned from the Battle of Buna with me. We rode a truck the thirty miles north into Brisbane with the baseball team (James as a spectator and me as a member of the team), and after the ball game decided we deserved a break. Our first sergeant, Master Sergeant Carr, one of the original National Guard members, could be a little bull-headed, and wouldn't give us a pass. We didn't think it was fair, so we decided to give ourselves a pass. Our timing wasn't real good, as we hadn't been paid in a while and we didn't have any money, so there wasn't really much we could do in the city. We slept at the Salvation Army, where we could get a free cot. The Red Cross had individual rooms, which were nicer, but we would've had to pay for those. When we got hungry, we went back to camp. Of course, I lost my sergeant stripes again, and was put on a wood cutting detail. But after chopping wood for just fifteen minutes on the first day of my punishment, I was released to play baseball.

*   *   *   *

Throughout the combat in New Guinea I came to expect death. I had buddies who were killed right next to me, and I killed enemy soldiers. Death doesn't get much closer than plunging your bayonet into an enemy soldier in front of you. We soldiers expected to be around death. What I didn't expect was news of death among the young on the home front, in my old neighborhood in Oklahoma City, affecting my sweetheart and next-door neighbors.

In one of those strange ironies of war, in August Leona's thirteen-year-old brother Jimmy was killed within two blocks of his home. Since Leona's mother worked the evening shift at Douglas Aircraft, Leona and her fifteen-year-old sister, Vera, were in the kitchen preparing supper for the family when it happened. Their dad was expected home from work soon. Jimmy had gone outside to tend to the family cow, which was grazing on vacant land near their house. When supper was about ready and Jimmy should've been back home, Vera went outside to get him. As she walked toward the vacant land, Vera saw an ambulance, and about fifty people standing around talking. She realized something big had happened in the neighborhood. As she pushed closer through the crowd, Vera saw Jimmy hanging by the neck from a tree. Screaming, Vera turned and ran back into the house. Between sobs, Vera told their father, who'd just come home from work, what she'd seen, and asked him to go cut Jimmy down. When she heard the news, Leona ran outside toward the scene, but my mother, who had just seen Jimmy's body, caught Leona by the arm and prevented her from getting near him. Leona often said that was a nice thing my mother did. Jimmy's feet were flat on the ground and his arms within reach of some branches, with a rope around his neck. He was dead. X-rays later revealed that his neck wasn't broken, but Jimmy had been strangled. The family never found out exactly what happened, but the police came to the house two days later and said, "It just looks like kids were playing and things got out of hand." They did no more investigating than that.

Leona remembered her little brother Jimmy as a blond, curly haired little boy. When Jimmy was just six or eight years old, he memorized songs he heard on the family's radio. He would sing one particular song over and over to guests, a lengthy song about four verses long called "Little Joe the Wrangler." Ironically, it was a story about a young Texas cowboy killed while wrangling cows. One time, when Leona's family had company, Jimmy was asked to sing his "Little Joe the Wrangler" song. She'll never forget the way Jimmy stood there, then finally said with great concentration, "I'll have to think it up," and then he sang all four stanzas.

*   *   *   *

Early in September 1943, I was confined to bed in one of the larger Brisbane hospitals, at Ascot Racetrack, for malaria and other jungle-related medical issues. This was one of the better hospitals, and the staff took good care of us. The veterans from New Guinea had black feet after spending so much time in the swamps. The nurses here were kind and tried to do what they could. They brought buckets of soap and water and tried their best to wash our feet clean, and couldn't understand why they remained black. One nurse wanted to use a brush on a soldier's feet, but he wouldn't let her. It just hurt too much. The stained feet were a lost cause. Our feet stayed that way for months. Only gradually did they begin to look normal again.

On Monday, September 13, 1943, while I was back at Camp Cable between outbreaks of malaria, we were told to march to an open area near a stage. The President's wife, Eleanor Roosevelt, had come to Brisbane as part of a five-week goodwill tour of the Pacific. She walked out on stage to a waiting microphone in front of thousands of soldiers, many of them combat veterans, and began to address the troops. The first thing out of her mouth was what great food we had. She'd not said ten words when the whole division booed her. The men were booing so long and so hard that she couldn't get another word out. When her handlers grasped the futility of continuing after that gaffe, she was put in a staff car and driven away. I think she'd been eating at the officer's mess, where, of course, they'd put on a good spread for her. I suppose it was insensitive of Mrs. Roosevelt to say what she did, but I blame the officers who were responsible for escorting her. Maybe she really thought all the men ate the same food as the officers did. Somebody should've told her otherwise. For booing the President's wife off the stage we were confined to base for two weeks, and given nothing to eat but cold beans and bully beef.

Not long after Mrs. Roosevelt's aborted speech, I was confined to bed at Ascot hospital, recuperating from malaria again, when my old company commander, Captain Sammy Horton, approached me. He was also being treated at Ascot for jungle-related problems at the time, but was on the mend, and was recruiting men to assist him with his new job. He'd been ordered back to New Guinea, where he would command the Army's jungle warfare school at Dobadura. He asked if I'd be interested in joining him as a jungle warfare instructor. I thought about it for a few seconds and said, "I don't believe I will." But that night I had a dream that I was back in battle in New Guinea and was shot in the buttocks. All the unwelcome memories of the Battle of Buna came rushing back to me. Knowing that MacArthur's army continued to battle the Japanese up the New Guinea coast, and expecting to join them again in the near future, I began to think that maybe being an instructor wouldn't be such a bad idea. So the next morning I went to his bedside and told Captain Horton I'd join him at the jungle warfare school after all. In order to have the authority needed to train the men, I was given sergeant stripes for the third time. This was in October 1943. A few weeks later saw the end of my service with the 32nd Infantry Division, but not the end of my participation on the division's ball team.

During my last game before leaving Australia, I caught the final out, a long fly ball caught over my left shoulder as I ran. But in making the catch, I ran so far back into center field that my feet got tangled up in a fence. Lieutenant Colonel McNabb and Lieutenant Colonel Miller, the same officers who sat on my court martial earlier in the year, produced a baseball bat, untangled the wire with it, and freed me. Baseball was really important to the 32nd Infantry Division in general, and their leaders in particular. They took pride in our winning record, and always treated the members of the team well. Even after I transferred to the jungle warfare school, the division's leadership flew me all the way back to Brisbane in a C-47 to play center field in the championships. We won the series and took the 1943 Australian title.

CHAPTER NINE:
JUNGLE WARFARE TRAINER

I arrived in Dobadura, New Guinea, in November 1943. I found that the jungle training camp, which included a population of approximately 1,500 students, trainers, and support personnel, was about a mile long, on a moderately flat piece of land that had been cleared by Army engineers. It was four to five miles from Dobadura Airfield, and a road had been built from the airfield to the training camp. Being back in New Guinea, so close to Buna, brought a return of unwanted memories, but teaching at the jungle school wasn't anything like fighting or living in the jungle as I'd known it a year before. Instructors and students alike slept on cots in tents, and there was a large wooden mess hall where cooks served us three meals a day.

I thought the training at the camp was pretty good. Sammy Horton, now Lieutenant Colonel Horton, I believe, as the commander, was in charge of the training. Each of the ten trainers was assigned about 125 men each, so there were something like 1,250 men being trained in jungle warfare at any one time. We kept each group about a month, though if they worked with us, they could get through the training faster. We taught soldiers new to New Guinea how to survive with minimal resources, what trees held the most water, which berries were edible, how to throw grenades in the jungle, and things like that. They would come in from Australia or directly from the States, as Milne Bay by this time had adequate dock facilities, and train with us for a month, then move up the coast to the north into combat.

Dobadura jungle training camp—open-air classrooms being built.

For a few weeks, training only on weekdays, we'd show the students training films, then throw some practical exercises at them and go over questions. If they just weren't getting it after that, we sent them to the field for a week of further instruction. When the Army required more men at the front, we sent the students on after only two or three weeks of training, working through the weekends. We didn't always know how much time we'd have with each class.

Once, I had a group of about thirty or forty men from the AAF who didn't think they needed jungle training, even after we showed them photos of dead Army Air Forces men who'd been overrun at Milne Bay the year before. We tried to get them to understand that in New Guinea "the front" or "the rear" didn't always exist as those concepts were normally understood. The enemy could make a landing anywhere, as Allied forces on New Guinea were normally located near the coast, plus enemy stragglers were often scattered in the jungle after a battle. I even told them the story of the red-haired AAF boy who had been used for bayonet practice. My AAF students failed to show much interest, so with LTC (Lieutenant Colonel) Horton's permission, I took them into the mountains and made sure they got lost for a few days. The problem was, I got lost myself, though the trainees never knew that. I left the trainees with two other trainers and went farther up a mountain to get my bearings, where I could see our camp in the distance. I then led the men back to camp. I think they got the message that, while they were stationed in New Guinea, there were a lot of ways they could find themselves in need of the skills we were trying to teach them. Later Sammy Horton just laughed about it.

My next batch of trainees included twenty-nine former criminals who'd been taken from prisons in the US, told that if they'd serve in the Army their records would be expunged. They were felons—bad characters who'd been imprisoned for every possible crime. At first, they were divided up equally so each trainer had two ex-prisoners in his group, but the other trainers didn't want anything to do with them, so LTC Horton gave them all to me. The other trainers had 125 regular soldiers. I had twenty-nine hardened convicts.

The very first morning of training, they all refused to fall out. So, I went after them. LTC Horton and a few of my fellow instructors were watching as I dragged an ex-con out of his tent in his shorts. I guess I picked the right guy, because after that I had no trouble with those boys. I often thought about them later and wondered how well they fought.

Initially, we were dependent on all our water being trucked in, perhaps from Dobadura. With such a high water table, I couldn't understand why the camp didn't have several wells of its own. Maybe it was just too new. In any case, my former prisoners dug a well for me in front of my tent. I could lower a three-gallon bucket with a rope to get water for washing and shaving. When the well was first dug, the water table was so high that water came up under pressure eight to ten feet, and we were worried it would flood the other tents, but after a few minutes it settled down to a couple feet below ground level. Two fifty-five gallon barrels with the ends cut off were placed down into the hole, and rocks and sand packed around the barrels. At first the water was really sandy, but after a day or two it cleared up. Eventually, one of the cooks had my well tested, and they began using it for drinking and cooking. The former prisoners also built three chairs, a table, and a platform for me to sleep on, and did other things for me. To everyone's surprise, we got along fine. For a while, I thought the guy I pulled out of the tent by his shorts would come after me at some point, but I never had any more problems with him. Usually, a tent like mine housed three or four men, but mine was laid out with chairs, a table, and eventually a refrigerator, so I had it all to myself.

Once LTC Horton found out I didn't mind taking the difficult trainees, he gave me more. At one point I was given a group of men who wouldn't train on certain days due to religious convictions. Some of them were Seventh Day Adventists who didn't want to train on Saturdays; I just let them make up Saturday by training on Sunday. The Jews were probably the most restrictive, though I never had more than four or five at a time, so they weren't a major problem.

Church service in New Guinea.

The camp often had inspirational and informative church services, in a fairly informal setup. We met out in the open, with the men sitting on logs, and we never knew what kind of chaplain would officiate. He could be from any Protestant denomination, or might be a Catholic priest. We didn't have chaplains assigned to the school, and I don't remember where these ministers/priests came from. They must've been on some type of rotation, probably from Dobadura or Port Moresby.

Officers occasionally ordered me to march my noncompliant troops to church services on Sundays, but I always refused. As a Christian, I believe if a person wants to go to church, he or she should go, but I don't think anyone should be forced. Whatever faith they were, Protestant, Catholic, Jewish, or something else altogether, when I was in charge I let my men worship on the day they wanted to, as their faith dictated. When Lieutenant Colonel Horton came to see why I wouldn't obey the order, I said, "Sammy," (I'd call him Sammy, even in front of the men), "I'm not going to force anyone to go to church. That just doesn't seem right." Sammy respected my point of view, and dropped the matter. Still, with all the restrictions these soldiers imposed on themselves, I often wondered what happened to them once they got into combat.

While I understood that combat doesn't wait for a certain day of the week, I was impressed with the depth of commitment to their faith these men had. It made me examine my own faith. If they were willing to contend against the system for their beliefs, even if I thought they were wrong, I had to ask myself how deep my commitment to God was. I did a lot of thinking, and that was really the beginning of a spiritual renewal for me, a watershed event in my life. I began to look at my commitment to Jesus Christ in a whole new way, not just trying to take the easiest path, but actually living the faith I professed, no matter how much it cost me. I wanted my faith to be something that went to the depth of my being, not just something I did for an hour or two on Sundays.

There were so many animals in the jungle surrounding our training camp that anyone who wanted to could have a pet fairly easily. I caught a parrot in the jungle and, even though I didn't tie it up, it seemed content to stay on a pole in my tent for days at a time. It would fly away for a few days, but always returned. I also had a friendly little monkey that liked everyone, except for one lieutenant. I suspect the lieutenant had once hit or kicked him, and the monkey didn't forget, because whenever the lieutenant came to my tent the monkey tried to bite him. Or, maybe the money sensed my aversion to lieutenants, and bit him out of sympathy for me. In any case, the monkey never bit anyone else.

As a sergeant, I was responsible for rationing beer and soda pop for the men we trained—they'd only get something like three cans per man, to last them the entire month they were in training. But with so many men coming and going, sometimes we'd have extra supplies on hand, because some men may have moved to the front early, before their ration was due. My ex-cons dug a platform and a hole, like a little cellar. I placed a cover over the cellar, with my cot over the cover. They put an old five-gallon dried potato tin in the hole, with copper tubing from a crashed Japanese Zero wound around inside it. The five-gallon tin could hold several cans of ABC beer, which was the brand issued by the Army. At this time we used aerosol mosquito bombs with Freon in them to kill mosquitos. Freon wasn't only the nation's foremost refrigerant, but also an effective mosquito/insect killer. I'd attach one of the Freon mosquito bombs to the copper tubing opening and pull the trigger. It worked quite well as a little makeshift refrigerator.

One day Lieutenant Colonel Horton came by to see me in my tent and said, "I know you've got a way to get cold beer out here in the jungle, but I don't know how. Let's see how you do it, Okie." So I pulled back the mosquito netting from over my cot, moved my cot to the side, and said, "Kick that dirt right over there." He did, and saw the cover, which he lifted to reveal the cellar with the whole setup. After that, every day LTC Horton came to my tent, and would say something like, "Okie, why don't you go see what's going on at the mess hall or something." While I was gone, he'd set off a Freon mosquito bomb and the homemade refrigerator would soon supply him with a cold beer. I suppose he drank two-thirds of the beer stored in the cellar, sitting in my tent day after day. Still, drinking the students' beer ration didn't diminish his reputation with me, as I remembered how he suffered with us during the Battle of Buna. I'll never forget him giving up his food ration for another man while we were all starving. Later, when LTC Horton and I left New Guinea on the same ship, the lieutenant colonel who replaced him ordered the makeshift cooler torn down, and reconstructed in <u>his</u> tent.

Though I was in Dobodura about nine months training troops on jungle warfare, part of that time was spent hospitalized for malaria. I stayed at a hospital in Dobodura once, and twice was flown to Port Moresby. Altogether, I was hospitalized at twelve different hospitals in New Guinea and Australia.

After training new troops in jungle warfare for about eight or nine months, I was fed up with not being able to go home, though I had twice the points needed. In World War II GIs rotated home based on points earned for time in combat zones and so forth. Soldiers required eighty-five points to go home, and I had over 200. Somehow I heard that the nearby 11th Airborne

Division at Buna was planning a parachute drop on Lae, New Guinea. The rumor was that the paratroopers who went on that dangerous mission (and made it through alive) could go home. Later I understood that none of that was true, as the 11th Airborne Division saw its first action in the liberation of the Philippines, and was only intensely training in New Guinea, conducting practice jumps, but at the time it seemed like a good idea to join them. Since we didn't have any trainees at the time, my friend Corporal Philip Dorn, a fellow jungle warfare trainer, and I left the jungle training camp and made our way to the 11th Airborne Division's airfield. Somehow we got our hands on a couple of parachutes, and made it on board an empty C-47 sitting on the ramp. We thought we were ready to go. I guess we must've told others back at camp that we were leaving to go jump with the airborne boys, because LTC Horton came looking for us. He drove up in a jeep and asked, "Just what are you two trying to do? I'm going home the same time you are, you know." Then he ordered us into the jeep, and drove back to camp. That was the end of my airborne career. I don't suppose many men went AWOL toward a battle, or what we thought would be a battle, so we didn't get into trouble. I don't know what we would've done had LTC Horton not driven up. We didn't have any weapons, or any of the right gear. We weren't really prepared to "hit the silk" with the airborne troops. We'd never had any parachute training. Even if the 11th Airborne was just preparing for a practice jump, I'm sure they'd never have let us jump with them. But we'd had enough; we weren't really thinking through the consequences at that point.

At 0900 one happy day, September 5 or 6, 1944, an officer drove into camp in a jeep with some big news. LTC Horton assembled all the jungle trainers for a meeting in the mess hall, and told us that most of the instructors were scheduled to ship out for home within the next few days. My name was on the list. Every man was a Buna combat veteran, and every man was injured or sick in some way. We were all ecstatic; it was a great feeling.

CHAPTER TEN:
GOING HOME...AND A BRIDE

I understand that waiting for a hospital ship delayed our trip home by about six months. But now it no longer mattered. All of us, including LTC Horton, left the Buna area on the 8th of September for Milne Bay and boarded a waiting hospital ship called the Sea Cat. The Sea Cat was a liberty ship, one of the mass-produced wonders of the war. I was in a multi-level hospital bunk most of the time, as only the seriously injured had single-high hospital beds. Nurses tended to me while I lay in the bunk—the first time in quite a while I'd seen American women. They kept mosquito nets over me, which didn't make a lot of sense to me since I'd had malaria for so long already, and besides, the mosquitoes that carried malaria were found in swamps, not on the open sea. I think they were afraid a stray mosquito would bite me and then carry malaria to others.

There were a lot of wounded men who remained in their beds for the entire voyage, but when I wasn't down with fever I could leave my bunk and roam the ship. I was so accustomed by this time to the periodic malaria episodes, and so happy to be going home, that it didn't bother me too much that I was coming home on a hospital ship. I'd rather not have had malaria, and I was often thoroughly miserable, but as I looked around the ship I saw a lot of men much worse off than me. I thanked God that I was going home at all.

Though I spent about two-thirds of the voyage in my bunk with malaria symptoms, I was told that when I was feeling better I was to report for KP duty in the officers' mess to peel potatoes. The number I peeled wouldn't have supplied mashed potatoes for a dozen men. I mainly explored the ship.

We sailed directly to the west coast of the USA, without putting into port anywhere along the way. On the 25th of September I had two birthdays when we crossed the International Date Line. The Navy cooks baked a little six inch cake for me; I must've told someone it was my birthday. Upon reaching the California coast, the Sea Cat headed for San Francisco Bay and I passed under the Golden Gate Bridge for the second time in my life—once sailing west, now sailing east. I thought back to that April night 2 ½ years ago when I stood on the deck of the Monterey. It seemed like a decade had passed. My life had been changed forever by the events that happened since I last passed under this bridge. I remember back in 1942 wondering how many of us would make it back, and how many would be killed. The Sea Cat was packed with wounded and sick men. I hadn't really thought there would be so many in that category.

The Sea Cat made a turn to port, passing Alcatraz prison, and docked at Angel Island, a small island in San Francisco Bay, that was now an Army processing center and prisoner of war camp, and until 1940 had been an immigration center. That took me by surprise, because, in my imagination anyway, I thought we'd dock at one of the many commercial or navy piers and be released on leave.

Those who could walk out under their own power, about half of the Sea Cat's patients, were ordered off the ship and assembled in front of some nearby wooden barracks. To our surprise, an officer stood on the barracks steps and announced that all of us would be quarantined in the barracks for two weeks. I looked around and saw that only enlisted men were present. The officers, LTC Horton included, had disembarked and disappeared. I guess the Army reasoned that only enlisted men could get communicable diseases.

We spent our quarantine sitting around, not doing much of anything, waiting. Immediately after our quarantine expired I was handed a set of orders with six names on it, mine included, and given train tickets for Kansas

City. We'd have to leave immediately. For the second time, I was in San Francisco but unable to see the sights.

Since I was the ranking man my job was to ensure the other five men arrived where they were supposed to go. Only the half dozen of us were not heading north—most of the guardsmen from the 32nd Infantry Division were heading back to Wisconsin and Michigan. The six of us traveled by cross-country train to Kansas City, and then on to Camp Chafee, Arkansas. There, I was given a Good Conduct Medal and a three-week pass to go home. With my pass in hand, I caught a bus from Fort Smith, Arkansas, to Oklahoma City.

I arrived in Oklahoma City on October 13, 1944, at two or three in the morning. Today, with the interstate, it's a 2 ½ hour trip from Fort Smith to Oklahoma City, but back then bus lines stopped at every town along the way, so the trip took some time. From the Oklahoma City bus station I took a cab to my parents' house on SE 38th street. My folks woke up when I knocked on the door, giving me a warm welcome, but I was tired and we agreed to talk after we all had some sleep.

As I was overseas corresponding with Leona, I eventually asked her to marry me. She said yes. Later, I found out she said yes to two or three other military men who were overseas like me. When I awoke on October 14, my first morning in Oklahoma City in two years and nine months, Leona was standing in the room. She'd come over to see me before she went to work. Leona later said the neighborhood was abuzz with my arrival, so she knew I'd come home. I was still groggy from my travels so we agreed to get together after she got off work. That was the first time we'd seen each other since I was drafted, and it was just for a few minutes. But we went out that night, dated for the three weeks I was home on leave, and talked about wedding arrangements. There was only one night we weren't together during that time. That was when Mom hosted a family reunion in my honor; it was wonderful to see all my aunts, uncles, and cousins who lived nearby again.

When I left for Australia, Leona was still in high school. In May 1943 she turned eighteen, and graduated from Capitol Hill High School the next month. She started nursing school just a few days after graduation, in an accelerated program at Mercy Hospital where the nurses in training lived on-site. All day she had real-world experience with patients on the floor, along with two hours a day of classroom instruction. Training continued seven days a week—no days off. In three months she earned her nurse's cap, which in peacetime would've taken six months. Much to Leona's distress, in November, after four months at Mercy Hospital, her mother made her quit the two-year RN program. Mrs. Nievar was very upset about an initiation ritual the twenty-five girls in her class were subjected to when they earned their caps. The frustrating thing for Leona was that she was already a month beyond the initiation by the time she told her mother about it, as she had no access to a phone and wasn't allowed to leave the premises. Yet her mother insisted she quit, even though it was past history. Leona loved all things medical, and found medical terminology, a foreign language to most of us, quite easy to pick up. She'd received straight A's on every test, and was really disappointed to have to leave the program. She tried everything she could to change her mother's mind, but to no avail. Leona won't talk about the initiation ritual to this day, except to say it did involve mild physical abuse. It must have been in bad taste, because two other girls left after the initiation, including a good friend of Leona's. So when I came home from the war, Leona was working as a receptionist at a chiropractor's office downtown.

All too soon my leave in Oklahoma City was up, and I boarded the train for Hot Springs, Arkansas. At Hot Springs I was issued new uniforms, as all mine had been stolen or lost on the trip home. In addition to my clothing, I lost the photo of Leona she'd sent me while I was in Australia, kangaroo-hide baseball shoes that were extra soft, a special kangaroo-hide baseball mitt, and a Japanese sniper rifle. I spent the first half of November 1944 at the Arlington Hotel in Hot Springs. It was luxury to me, with maid service, bellhops, table waiters, and entertainment of all kinds. I had a daily medical checkup, military records reviews, and classes an hour or two a day. Of course I enjoyed it, since it was so unlike the Army I had known, but I wanted to get home to Oklahoma City and Leona very badly. It was hard to be back in the States and so close to home but not be able to see Leona, to whom I was now very eager to marry.

On November 9th I was classified 3C due to malaria and jungle rot in my feet, which meant limited duty in the States for at least six months. I requested duty close to home at Fort Sill, but on the 14th of November 1944, I received orders for Camp Plauche (pronounced "Pla-Shey"), near New Orleans. I was hoping I'd get a furlough to come home to marry Leona, but it was wartime and I was at the mercy of the Army bureaucracy. In the end, the furlough didn't come through, but I was crazy about Leona and traveled to Oklahoma City anyway, "on the way" to New Orleans.

I arrived home Thursday evening, the 16th of November. Leona and I went out that evening and discussed what we would do. We knew we wanted to get married, but we were very constrained by the reality of our wartime situation. We decided it had to be now. We had no idea when we'd be together again, as we didn't know where the Army would send me. We didn't know what the future held, but we did know we wanted to face it together. That very night we went to the homes of a preacher and then an employee of the courthouse, people who friends had told us might be able to handle a last-minute wedding. Both of them turned us down—it was 10:00 or 11:00 PM after all. Maybe they thought we were crazy. I guess we were really crazy… crazy in love.

The next morning I went next-door to Leona's house and we took a city bus to the courthouse to get a marriage license. I left my Chevrolet at my parent's home as I was planning to go directly to the downtown train station after getting married downtown and spending a few hours together. We didn't tell our parents a thing, as they'd probably think we were crazy too. Leona worried, as she waited for me to arrive that morning, that her mother would wonder why she hadn't gone to work at the chiropractor's office. But her mother had worked the night shift at Douglas Aircraft and slept through it—Leona had told her younger brothers and sisters to keep quiet. Leona's mother had purchased the material for a nice blue velvet dress and wanted us to get married at Draper Park Christian Church. We would've liked that too, but we just didn't have time. Leona would later use the material to make the dress she wore when we had the chance to have our wedding picture taken in December.

At the Oklahoma County Court House, a court clerk approached us and asked, "Do you have any plans on where you want to be married?" We said, "Not necessarily. What do you suggest?" He informed us a judge could marry us in his chambers, so we went to Judge Carl Traub's chambers and were married by him on Friday, November 17, 1944, at 10:00 AM. Leona's maid of honor was a friend named Betty who worked at the chiropractor's office with Leona. Since the chiropractor's office was just two blocks from the courthouse, Betty was able to walk down to meet us. The court clerk stood in as my best man. I didn't even have time to ask one of my brothers.

I had to leave for New Orleans at 3:00 PM. We just had a matter of hours together. Betty very kindly offered us the keys to her house, several miles away, so we could be alone. That was our honeymoon.

Before we left the courthouse, we called our folks to break the news. My father was at work, but my mom was home and wasn't too happy with us getting married. She thought I'd come home from the war and help take care of her (with her cancer). She also didn't want anyone to take her boy away. I thought I'd done my part to help the family, as during the war I faithfully sent money home, and bought my folks a car. Later I heard that my father was fine with the whole thing. We then called Leona's mother, knowing her father was, like my father, at work. When Leona got off the phone she said her mother was angry, but I thought she'd get over it. After some drama when Leona returned home, her mother did get over it, with the help of Leona's cousin Wanita, who got her "Aunt Rosie" to think clearly again. Leona's dad liked me and I never had any problems with him. There were thousands of couples like us tying the knot during the war, and none knew what the future held. Few had the time they really wanted to plan a proper wedding. A lot of people thought we were crazy. I guess we weren't so crazy after all, because as of this writing we're a month and a half from our sixty-fifth wedding anniversary.

It was a sad parting at the train station. We'd been married only five hours. I was AWOL, as I'd been given a day to travel to New Orleans, and obviously didn't make it. When I arrived at Camp Plauche, New Orleans, and reported to the first sergeant, I thought I'd get into some trouble for sure, even though I told him the story of our wedding. However, he didn't care at all, and said he really didn't have anything for me to do. He told me to report each morning for guard duty, but after a couple of hours I was free to go. I rode around in a jeep with another guard—he had a rifle and I had a pistol, and didn't do a whole lot. Since I had a license to drive just about any Army vehicle, sometimes they'd have me move a tank or a big truck to another location on base. I was really just waiting for a more permanent assignment. At this time, I also thought I might be getting out of the Army soon. That was a good reason not to move Leona to Louisiana. But there was another reason. I didn't give much thought to bringing Leona to Camp Plauche because a married soldier was only allowed two passes a week to see his wife. It was very difficult to be separated from my new bride.

Not long after returning to the States, I found that the heavy wool winter issue uniforms made my skin break out. I was given a letter from an Army doctor stating that I was to wear the lightweight summer issue uniforms called "suntans." Still, it was winter so I was frequently harassed for wearing the wrong uniform. I don't know why my skin broke out with the wool, but it had something to do with my service in the jungles of New Guinea.

At Camp Plauche, I was again classified 3C, with orders not to do any marching, walking, or drilling, as the jungle rot in my feet gave me trouble after marching or walking for more than a few minutes. An Army doctor bet me a box of cigars I'd be out of the Army and home by Christmas. In fact, personnel clerks told me there was no use completing an allotment to have money sent to my new wife, since I'd be out of the Army before it started. Thankfully, I didn't trust them, and filled out the allotment paperwork anyway. The personnel office also checked my records and found I was supposed to have the Combat Infantryman Badge, which would earn me another $10 a month—very welcome for a new groom. But like everything in the Army, it would take time. First they had to write to the 32nd Infantry Division and confirm my combat service. You'd think my personnel records would already reflect all that.

While at Camp Plauche, I attended classes every day on the changes that had taken place in the States while I was overseas and watched films about army life, ninety percent of which I knew from experience was nonsense. There were also the usual films on venereal disease and so forth. They really were just wasting time until they found a job I could do with my feet problems, or released me from the Army. On the positive side, it was at Camp Plauche that I saw Sergeant Dorn again, my buddy from the New Guinea jungle training school who slipped aboard the airborne division's C-47 with me.

The first week of December I was given a pass to make a quick trip to Oklahoma City, but after that I was just as lonely as ever for my new bride. I returned to Camp Plauche at 1000 on December 8, thirteen hours late. Fortunately, I'd asked a conductor on one of the trains to provide a note explaining the late trains that caused the delay, and the Army overlooked it. In the second week of December, 1944, the Army decided we needed to learn to load, aim, and fire a rifle, as well as how to throw grenades. Given my combat and jungle combat trainer experience in the Pacific Theater, this nonsensical training really annoyed me. My frustration was short-lived though, as not long into that training I received word that my Aunt Lena died, and I was allowed to go home on leave for the funeral. I was finally able to spend a little time with my new bride.

Robert & Leona's wedding photo, a month and a half after their wedding - December, 1944.

I returned to Camp Plauche on January 6, 1945, to find that they were teaching the company to tie different types of knots. I was tired of this foolishness, and ready for the Army to make a decision on my status. Some of the boys rated 1-A were heading back out to the Pacific. These were men who'd already been overseas once, but didn't have as much time overseas as I had, and were healthier than I was.

Eventually, Leona joined me and we rented a single room with no kitchen, so we had to have our meals out. One night we'd eat fried oysters and the next night we'd have spaghetti, alternating between those two meals, because they were both only fifty cents a plate at a nearby diner. Surprisingly, Leona still likes fried oysters and spaghetti. After about a month, we rented another room in an old house that had been divided into several living quarters. It was great to be together, but life wasn't easy as a new Army couple. We had a three-burner coal-oil cook stove in our room, but only one burner worked until Leona got a second going. We had a card table as our "kitchen" table, but no kitchen. The card table was bowed in the middle, so we set a gravy bowl in the center. To wash dishes we left our room, went out via the porch to another entrance, and climbed the stairs to use the faucet in the second floor bathroom. Then back down with the water. We lived there another month, then moved right next door, with a much better setup. There, we had a proper kitchen, or should I say four of us couples shared a kitchen. We had our own bedroom, but shared a bathroom with the other three couples. We were in that house another three or four months.

At one point, Leona had a bad urinary tract infection and was admitted to the base hospital overnight. The doctor ordered a retrograde pylogram to determine the problem and pronounced that Leona would probably have to have a kidney removed. Thankfully, later the doctor decided other treatment should suffice. We were very thankful for the latter diagnosis, especially since Leona never had any more problems.

Finally the Army, in their wisdom, decided not to discharge me, but that I'd make a good typist. As I was playing baseball long before players started wearing baseball gloves, all my fingers were jammed or broken and my hands are broad and definitely not delicate. I flunked out of typing school in a week. Then I was assigned to yet another school that was so unremarkable I can't even remember what specialty it was. I didn't pass that one either. Ultimately, they put me in charge of German Prisoners of War (PWs) in Texas.

Thus, in March 1945 I was assigned to Camp Maxey, near Paris, Texas, northeast of Dallas, just south of the Oklahoma border. I went down to Texas alone, while Leona traveled from Louisiana to Oklahoma to visit her family. After a week away, Leona joined me and we rented a house from a Mrs. Scott.

When I first arrived, Camp Maxey consisted of one camp, or area. Many of the German PWs worked on local farms, or in camp doing the laundry, policing up, cooking, etc. I often saw truckloads of Germans standing in the beds of Army trucks on their way to or from nearby farms to work. I never heard of any of those prisoners escaping. But soon after I arrived, a new camp was completed for elite Waffen SS (Schutz Staffel) troops and prisoners who refused to work. I was put in charge of the approximately thirty to forty guards at the new camp with the difficult prisoners; it was called Area 18. I don't know why they put me in charge of Area 18. Maybe because they knew I had combat experience and had taught jungle warfare, including a period when I oversaw a group of difficult ex-prisoners. My boss, Captain Kent, spent most of his time at the other camp, so Area 18 was run by NCOs. We would normally see Captain Kent only once a week. The main camp had 8,000-10,000 prisoners; the smaller camp where I worked had 1,500. In the larger camp, when the prisoners were off base, one guard could handle sixty German PWs, but it was one-for-one with the SS troops from our camp. Since they refused to work, the SS men didn't leave camp very often, but every once in a while they had to, to visit the hospital or something.

One time, one of our soldiers fell out of a jeep and hit his head, sustaining a serious injury. The only doctor near the post who could perform the surgery was an SS neurosurgeon, who initially refused because he was afraid for his life. In his country he could've been shot if the surgery proved to be unsuccessful, so he was afraid to attempt it. He insisted a release be signed so he wouldn't be held responsible for any unfavorable results. Since the GI was unconscious, his parents had to be brought in to give their permission. A field was cleared so the parents' plane could land right at the camp, and we billeted them in the guards' barracks. The parents did give their permission, the SS surgeon performed the surgery, and it was successful. The soldier was up and around before too long.

I worked twenty-four hours straight, then had twenty-four hours off, then pulled twenty-four hour alert, which was just like working since there was always something bad going on. It was my job to schedule the guards to ensure adequate manning for our six guard towers and the main gate, ideally to have two men to a tower and three or four men on the main gate. We counted the prisoners twice a day, every morning and night. All the prisoners working at our camp, cooking and policing up, came from the larger camp, as the SS troops refused to work. Seeing all these prisoners everywhere really perplexed me, as in New Guinea the Japanese, as a rule, would never surrender, no matter how untenable their positions became. It amazed me that their allies obviously surrendered in droves. I learned later that by the time I arrived at Camp Maxey, German prisoners were arriving in the United States at the rate of 50,000 <u>a month</u>, yet after three years of war the <u>total</u> number of Japanese prisoners of war in US hands was less than two thousand.[1]

Some of my guards' records duly recorded that they weren't to carry firearms. They'd seen too much of the horrors of war, and at times had problems behaving appropriately. One guard, Private Metusic, killed a rabbit with a machine gun, in the process sawing through an entire 12" x 12" guard post with the bullets. He then left his post, picked up the very dead rabbit, and took it to the kitchen for the cooks to prepare. Captain Kent couldn't punish him because Metusic's records showed that he wasn't to handle fire-arms, yet the Army made him a guard at an SS PW camp anyway. I wasn't about to have an unarmed guard, with the SS on the other side of the wire. Nevertheless, when Private Metusic was on duty, he'd often open fire with his machine gun—at what, I have no idea. When I heard the bullets flying, I'd just lie flat until he quit shooting. In ten minutes he'd be back to normal. Leona also heard him firing many times when she was visiting the camp, and would lie flat on the ground, too. One time an officer asked, "What's he do-ing here anyway?" I replied, "You guys gave me these men. I don't know." Private Metusic loved animals, and one night coming back from town he brought four dogs with him, and put them in his room in the barracks, as he said, "Just to get them out of the rain."

Private Jenkins was another guard who'd start firing a machine gun at times. He was a real decent guy when he wasn't having flashbacks, but he'd seen too much combat in Italy. I thought these guys made pretty good guards, because the SS troops were scared of them and stayed away from the wire.

One night, an American lieutenant from the main camp wandered over to Area 18 drunk, and ordered me to have my men fall out. He wanted us to conduct close order drill in front of the German SS prisoners' barracks, just to show his authority. I refused, until he had those dismissed who weren't to handle a rifle or were crippled from the war and couldn't march. After he agreed, I lined up the men. There were only three men remaining. The lieu-tenant got mad and stomped off. The next morning I reported the incident to Captain Kent, and the lieutenant never came back.

One of the German prisoners from Camp 19 was George Schmeling, Max Schmeling's brother. Max Schmeling was a well known boxer, the heavyweight champion of the world from 1930-1932. George Schmeling was in charge of garbage pickup at both camps, and helped me out by ensuring the SS prisoners didn't get near the gate while we opened it for him to make his pickup.

One day while counting the prisoners, I found dirt under the cots of one barracks building, and under the barracks' floorboards, so we knew the SS troops were digging an escape tunnel. We watched what was going on until we figured the tunnel was a few feet from the perimeter fence. I then doubled the guard with extra machine guns at the point we expected to see the tunnel opening emerge, ready to "let 'em have it." Just as we approached what we anticipated would be the big day, it rained heavily and the tunnel caved in. That was a good thing for the Germans, because their tunnel would've emerged right next to Private Metusic's tower. I questioned the SS troops as to who dug the tunnel, but they wouldn't talk. So, I assigned one PW barracks each day to work on filling in the tunnel. I have no idea why the Germans were digging a tunnel with the war just about over, except they were SS, true-believer Nazis. Even so, I don't think most of the men wanted to escape—they were probably driven to it by a few of their officers. Our camp had separate officer and enlisted barracks for the SS troops, but they were all within the same fence.

The Germans were quite creative. They'd collect the wooden crates their fruit came in, and make things with the wood. One of the Germans made a beautiful violin, and all he wanted for payment was a carton of cigarettes. Since I didn't smoke, I had to go buy some, and by the time I returned with the cigarettes, he had the violin sold to someone else. One of them did make me a little box with a matching lid, which was very well crafted considering what they had to work with. Again, all he wanted in payment was some cigarettes, which apparently was the standard PW currency.

Wooden box made by German SS prisoners at Camp Maxey, Texas.

One day, Leona planned a trip to the commissary and the hospital at the other camp. Area 18 didn't have such luxuries. After leaving the commissary with her groceries, she walked over to the mess hall and saw someone working there. Leona asked, "Would you please put these perishables in the refrigerator while I go by the hospital to pick up some medicine?" Nothing. The man didn't understand her. Then he started speaking in German, which gave her a fright. Soon the American sergeant in charge of the mess hall came over and took care of things. Leona didn't realize the mess hall workers were German prisoners; I think she was surprised to be so up close and personal with the enemy, with them being right out in the open. Sometimes, Leona would come out to Area 18 when I was on duty and we'd sit on the grass and play cards. When she came to see me, Leona often walked close to the PW fence, but the prisoners never whistled at her like Americans would. They were probably afraid of being machine-gunned by Private Metusic.

My assistant, Staff Sergeant Kaiser, actually outranked me, as I was still a Sergeant, but for some reason I was put in charge of all the guards. Perhaps my most important helper was Corporal Jim Mortenson from Wisconsin, a former truck driver who weighed about 200 pounds, and could handle himself well. We became good friends, and Leona and I later visited Jim and his wife, Florence, in Wisconsin five or six times after the war.

On May 8, 1945, Germany surrendered, and the war in Europe was over. When we got the news I doubled the guard. I was afraid there'd be trouble with our SS prisoners when they heard they had lost the war. I didn't go home to Leona that night. Thankfully, all was quiet. These men were so hard-core we also thought they might take the news as US propaganda. They'd soon see that wasn't the case.

By July 1945, Leona was pregnant with our first child, Trish. Trish's birth ended up costing a grand total of $25, since she was conceived while I was still in the Army, and they paid the bills. Newborn Trish would weigh in at just a little over five pounds. That's only five dollars a pound—a real bargain.

On August 6 the AAF dropped a nuclear bomb on Hiroshima, and three days later one on Nagasaki. On August 15, Japan announced its unconditional surrender. World War II was finally over. By the 22nd of August, only 2,500 German PWs were left at Camp Maxey, with more leaving every week, beginning the journey back to their homeland.

After another trip to Oklahoma City together, I returned to Texas while

Leona stayed in Oklahoma City, anticipating that I'd be discharged soon. The war was over and my Army service was winding down. I was eager to get out of the Army and start a new life.

Even with the pressures of guarding the often uncooperative SS prisoners, I played baseball when I could. At one point, a combined team, from Areas 18 and 19, was flown to Abilene, Texas, for a state-wide tournament. We won second place.

Shortly after we returned from Abilene, we began to prepare to move our SS troops to Arizona, and in late August we transported 200 prisoners by train. Our train collected an additional 300 prisoners and their guards in Fort Worth, and at Sweetwater another 300 from Camp Hood; eventually there were about twenty-five cars in the train with 1,200 prisoners. Our two hundred prisoners took up three of the cars. Most of the guards from Area 18 came with us, and Corporal Mortenson and I went through each car and counted the men every time the train stopped. Our orders were simply to take the prisoners to Tucson, Arizona. I have no idea why. It seemed to me transporting them east instead of west would've been a better first leg on their journey back to Europe.

When we returned, Camp Maxey was now devoid of German prisoners, but there was still a lot of uncertainty as to when we'd all be discharged. I knew it would be soon. Everyday I waited expectantly, hoping to get some news. I was able to get a two-day pass to Oklahoma City, and made it back to Camp Maxey at midnight on September 12, just an hour before I had to be on guard duty. The trip back took me twelve hours, catching a Butter Krust bread truck to Pauls Valley, another commercial truck to Davis, yet another to Ardmore, and three more rides to Paris, Texas, arriving at 2330. To finish the journey I caught a bus to Camp Maxey, arriving at midnight. I had to be on duty at 0100. That was cutting it close. I didn't really have anyone to answer to, but it was important to me as the leader to be an example to my men. I didn't want anyone working extra hours to cover for my absence.

At this time, I heard my old buddy, Bob Teeples, had received a battlefield promotion. He went straight from staff sergeant to captain, becoming the commander of L-Company, my old company, after I left the 32nd Infantry Division. I was real happy to hear that, and I'm sure Bob made a good officer.

Though he could see my happiness at the prospect of being discharged,

Captain Kent tried to talk me into staying in the Army. I said, " I will, if you make me a first sergeant." He didn't have the authority to do that, so that was it for my Army career. By early September Camp Maxey had been made into a discharge camp, meaning outgoing GIs weren't forced to travel to another Army post to be discharged. By the 19th of September my unit was discharging just two men a day, but on September 22 I received my discharge orders. I had a medical screening on September 25 and heard some speeches, then was happily discharged from the Army on September 26, 1945, three years and eight months after being drafted. It was the day after my twenty-ninth birthday. I thought it was a wonderful birthday present.

My mess tin, which is one of the few things I carried throughout the war and brought home, originally just read "U.S. 1918 BA. CO" on the bottom. With my bayonet I scratched the names of places I passed through on the side. Some of these places aren't even on the map.

USA
Fort Sill, Camp Roberts, Fort Ord, San Francisco

AUSTRALIA
Adelaide, Woodside, Melburn (sic), Sidney, Newcastle, Brisbane, Camp Cable, Townsville

NEW GUINEA
Port Moresby, Owen Stanley Range, Wanigela, Abau, Segili, Umisi, Lakwa, Sinaipara, Wapopo, Gobi, Emo Mission, Ora Bay, Embogu, Dobodura, Sinemi, Cape Endaiadera, Buna, Sanananda, Milna Bay, Goodenough Island

Somewhere along the way I was awarded two Bronze Stars for my actions in New Guinea. I have the medals to this day, and photographs of them are on the back cover of this book. My discharge certificate lists them as part of my official records. But with my personnel file having been lost in the 1973 fire at the National Personnel Records Center in St. Louis, I don't even remember for what specific actions they were awarded.

EPILOGUE

Trying to pick up a normal life after the war wasn't easy. My first 4th of July after becoming a civilian again just about drove me crazy. All the fireworks and explosions were hard to take. I'd had enough explosions and loud noises to last me a lifetime.

For some time after the war, whenever anyone spoke of not harming another person or particularly of not killing, it bothered me inside. I've been blessed with having Baptist and Christian Church ministers who were sensitive to the needs of veterans returning from our nation's wars, and were true patriots. However, some of the revival preachers I heard in various places really disturbed me. I tried to remind myself that when they spoke against killing or harming others, they weren't talking about me, but I couldn't help it; I struggled with guilt. I knew in my heart that when I killed other men in New Guinea, I was only protecting my country, doing my job, but I did feel guilty for years after the war. I think a large part of it was the close, personal, nature of the fighting, man-on-man, that I experienced. I had to go right into bunkers and kill other men up close, to smell their sweat and their blood, and at times to look them in the eyes as I violently ended their lives. Sometimes I killed wounded men. It was brutal, nasty business. I wish I hadn't had to do it. I reminded myself that the Japanese would never have surrendered peaceably, and there was no other way for the Allies to rid the Pacific of their evil regime, a regime that had attacked the US and enslaved most of Asia.

I still set off airport security alarms with the metal in my leg from the bullet fragments (or fragments from my rifle) that lodged there after my M1 rifle was shot from my hands. Years after the war, I was visiting the US Capitol in Washington, D.C. and set off a security alarm. Leona won't walk with me through department store alarms, as I set those off, too. It embarrasses her to watch them shake down an old man. It wasn't until May 2009, while seeing my orthopedic physician, that I finally had an x-ray done. Sure enough, a radiologist found the two pieces of metal lodged in my left leg from the battle more than sixty-six years before.

I'm still not over the malaria I picked up in the jungles of New Guinea. Malaria is a miserable illness. At times, I'm freezing and burning up at the same time. When I have an attack, I get a 103-104 degree temperature, and sweat just pours off me like water. It's happened every year since the war, including as recently as March 2009. When I was discharged from the Army, I was given big bottles of 1,000 tablets of quinine, and more bottles of atabrine. I didn't get a VA disability, but I'm eligible for treatment at the VA hospital anytime I need it. However, it's not worth it; I typically spend all day sitting around waiting. The jungle rot still flares up, too, in little white strips in the creases of my face and on my feet, more than six decades after the war. The VA has given me cortisone and dermatologists have tried a few things, but they've never cured it. They can only make it better for a while.

While I was in the dark jungles of New Guinea, I decided that if I somehow made it out alive I wanted to live in the city so I could always see the city lights at night. I do live in the city to this day, just a few miles from downtown Oklahoma City. We live close enough that on April 19, 1995, when Timothy McVeigh and Terry Nichols destroyed the Alfred P. Murrah Federal Building with a truck bomb, Leona and I could hear the blast. The aluminum front door rattled and glass shook in our home. I was sitting in my chair, reading a newspaper, when it happened. Leona said there must be someone knocking at the front door. Recognizing the sound, without lowering my newspaper I said, "No, it's a bomb." Leona didn't believe me. Thirty minutes later, our daughter-in-law called and asked if we could watch our grandson, as she was a nurse and all nurses had been summoned to area hospitals.

As of this writing, September 2009, I'm ninety-three years old, and Leona and I have been married almost sixty-five years. We bought a house in 1947 just a few blocks from where we lived as next-door neighbors before the war, and live there to this day. Leona and I had four children—Trish-1946, Jean-1949, Michael-1953, and David-1954. Baby Michael died in childbirth, and golden-haired Jean died in 1959 at age ten of a brain tumor. We have eight grandchildren and four great-grandchildren.

Leona tells a wonderful story from the time Michael was born, to his passing shortly thereafter, when God comforted her in a special way during a time of intense sorrow. Early in the night, when Leona was in labor, she found herself alone in the hospital room. I was in the waiting room, with Leona's sister Lillian. In those days, family members were expected to wait there until the baby was born. A little bedside table next to Leona had a lamp and a little Bible on it. Leona just naturally picked up the Bible and opened it. It fell to John 14:2-3, where Jesus said "In my Father's house are many mansions: if it were not so, I would have told you. I go to prepare a place for you. And if I go and prepare a place for you, I will come again, and receive you unto myself; that where I am, there ye may be also." Just then the nurse entered and said, "Oh honey, this light is not bright enough for you to read by; you need to rest. You try to go back to sleep." Later that night, I think about midnight, Michael was born. Leona was medicated because she had eclampsia, a potentially life-threatening complication of pregnancy. She wasn't aware of any problems with Michael. She thought it was a normal birth and a healthy child. The doctor told me that Michael was born without the left side of his diaphragm, and just forty-five minutes into his life, he died. When Leona awoke, the doctor told her Michael was gone. Throughout the immediate trial and then later in life, Leona often considered Jesus' words in John 14. We know where Michael is. Leona has gained great comfort knowing that someday she's going to hold him again. We don't know why Michael died then, but we do know God gave Leona a very comforting gift that gave her the strength to carry on. She has asked that John 14:2-3 be read at her funeral.

My mother survived her cancer and lived another thirty-five years to enjoy her eleven grandchildren. She was known for her green thumb. She could stick a rose branch in the ground and it would sprout a new rose bush. Roses and peonies brought by her grandmother from Missouri when she moved to Oklahoma City many years before circled my Mom's property in flowerbeds. I brought some of those same peonies to our own flower beds, and our daughter Trish then took a few back to Missouri for her flower bed. They've now gone full circle.

As soon as I was discharged from the Army, I went to work in the glass business, like my father, at ACME Glass. In 1949 I made a change to Pittsburgh Glass, working mostly big high-rise jobs. For a nine-year stretch I worked in Stillwater, Oklahoma, Monday through Friday, and came home to Oklahoma City on weekends. I spent my whole career in the glass business, ending up at Knox Glass, from which I retired in 1987.

I guess fitness in old age runs in the family—my grandfather was killed in an automobile accident at age 91 while he was out on a date. At the age of 72, I taught three of my grandchildren how to walk on stilts. I played baseball or softball until I was 88 years old, when I was on a championship "Over 70's" team. I played softball with my son, David, in an Oklahoma City men's league into the late 1990's; they'd put me in the game if the team didn't have enough players. The league was composed mainly of young men 20-30 years old. While I couldn't run the bases like I used to, I could still hit as well as most of the others.

Sometime after the war I got into coaching. When David was in grade school in the 1960's I coached his team, and in the 1970's I coached a Draper Park Christian Church (DPCC) women's softball team. It started out as a way for the ladies to get some exercise, but they worked hard and ended up becoming pretty good and playing in a city league. Several of the ladies are DPCC members to this day.[1]

After I was discharged from the Army and we settled down in Oklahoma City, we alternated between my family's Baptist church and Leona's Christian church. However, after our first child, Trish, was old enough to attend Sunday School, Leona insisted on taking her to Draper Park Christian Church. If all three of us went to Sunday School at the Baptist church, Leona and I wouldn't be able to sit together, as men and women had separate classes. From about 1948 to January 1959, I attended a Baptist church on Sundays while attending class parties and other social events with Leona at Draper Park Christian Church. I got to know the people at DPCC and made a lot of friends.

Draper Park Christian Church started in 1928 as an independent

Christian church on Broadway Avenue, across from Draper Park in southeast Oklahoma City, just west of where we live now, and Leona lived then. Draper Park Christian Church is associated with other independent Christian churches in the Restoration Movement, which are simply churches that seek to return to first century Christianity, free of the extrabiblical culture, tradition, and additional rules and regulations that have crept into the Church over the centuries. DPCC was modeled after the early churches described in the New Testament, with spiritual authority held by men called Elders, and the practical work of the church overseen by Deacons. Their motto is, "Where the Scriptures speak, we speak; where the Scriptures are silent, we are silent." They have a deep love and respect for God's Word.

When Leona was young, she and most of her nine brothers and sisters would walk to church, but her three youngest siblings didn't have decent clothes to wear, so they had to stay home. That's how it was in the Depression. It's hard today to even imagine a child staying home because he or she couldn't come up with even one set of decent clothes. Though Leona's family initially attended a nearby Methodist church, a wonderful next-door neighbor, DPCC Sunday School teacher Clarence Lowry, invited Leona's sister to Draper Park, and then started taking Leona. Soon, the whole family was attending. In April 1937, Leona was baptized by the DPCC minister, Harold Stine.

In January 1959 I made a deal with Leona. I'd attend Draper Park Christian Church if she quit teaching Sunday School so we could be together. She agreed. Back then, Draper Park had about 150 members, and still met in that white wooden structure on Broadway near Draper Park.

One event will always stand out in our minds about Draper Park Christian Church. When we were down, when we really needed our Christian brothers and sisters, they were there for us. We'll never forget that. In 1959, our beautiful, golden-haired Jean suffered a serious illness that was very difficult for our family, and culminated in her death on November 1, 1959. It took the doctors some time to determine what was wrong with her, and in July 1959 she underwent exploratory surgery. The surgeon found a glioma, or tumor, that was wrapping itself around her brain stem. The doctors said it was inoperable.

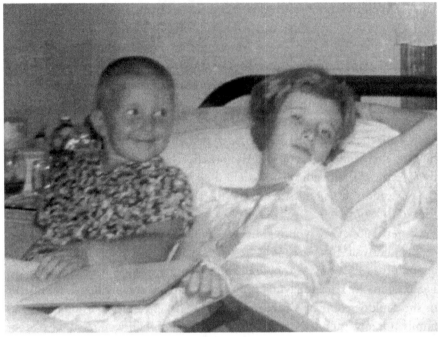

Jean, sick in bed, being visited by her brother David.

Because of Leona's medical training we were able to take Jean home and care for her there until her death. Her care was very expensive, and our insurance coverage didn't extend to home care. A Christian neighbor named Walt Hague went door-to-door throughout the neighborhood and raised $400. The people of Draper Park Christian Church presented us with a gift of $700, a lot of money back then. People came to clean, cook, and do anything they could. Not just for a few days, but for months. The minister and his wife would come by and always seemed to say just the right things to encourage us. Every week, Marvel Fish would bring her own bucket and mop. She'd come in quietly, mop the kitchen, and then leave—every week. On Sundays, Harold and Eugenia Short came by to visit. Irene Prior showed Christian love by helping with the housework. Fanny and Lee Ransom would visit with Jean and the family. One member of DPCC was a nurse who would come to place a catheter. The last month of Jean's life was exhausting. Leona's mother stayed up all night with Jean so Leona could get some sleep. Harold Short's mother and many others brought us food. Many times. Diane Arnold came at least three times a week and spent all day cooking, cleaning, washing dishes, and doing the laundry. Eugenia Short kept Diane's three children so Diane would be free to do this. Diane's husband, Harley, and many other members—more than I can name or remember—came by to check on us and make sure we were all right. I saw Christianity demonstrated through people's actions. I saw the true love of Christ in these people. I saw Christ, Himself, in them. I wanted to be part of living out that walk with God with these people. And so, I moved my membership to Draper Park Christian Church. In the 1960s, I was a Deacon, and then an Elder. We still attend Draper Park Christian Church. Leona has been a member for 72 years now, and is recognized as the longest-running continual (except for a matter of months during World War II) member.

<u>Final note from Bob and Leona's daughter Trish</u>
I know World War II changed the lives of all who experienced it. But some would also suffer physically the rest of their lives. I remember coming home from school one day as a young child and finding my daddy at home and in bed. I didn't know it then, but he was suffering a malaria attack. My daddy never intentionally missed a day of work except for my brother's funeral, and later, my sister's funeral. He was a lot of fun, but he was a "man's man." He had huge weight-lifter arms and a very small waist. My mother would have to alter size 44 suit coats for him in the waist, and the arms would still be tight. He lifted 400 to 500 pound plate glass windows with one man on the other end of the plate. To find my daddy in bed made me feel frightened and helpless. He just lay there, sweating from the fever. Quinine and aspirin were all he had. He just had to sweat it out.

Though Oklahoma winter weather is fairly mild, it can also be bitter, with below freezing temperatures, and there's no doubt Oklahoma gets more than its share of ice storms. Yet, even in bitter cold, my daddy would always go to work, in hopes that the crews would be allowed to work at least part of the day. Some days, the foremen would say it was too dangerous to handle heavy glass, or climb several stories up a building carrying glass on the ice. If Daddy stayed out in that weather all day, he would come home at night with fingers frozen. We waited to have dinner while he sat in his rocker, thawing out. I felt sorry for him, even as a small child. I hated snow as a child, because I knew my daddy would have to work outside in it. He never said a word, of course.

The Santa Clause in him comes out every Christmas. Once, when I was a child, my parents bought us a slide, back when slides were free standing metal toys. When we awoke Christmas morning and walked into the living room, we saw Daddy was more excited than we were. I don't know how he could stay up until midnight assembling toys, and then be so energetic on Christmas morning. He insisted on showing us how to climb to the top and slide down, and sure enough, he was the first one. He slid right into the glass coffee table. The coffee table shattered into a million pieces, and we children froze...until Daddy threw back his head and laughed. We children covered our mouths and giggled softly. He loved to hand out the gifts on Christmas morning. And as we opened them, he would show us how each worked. I've seen this big, muscular man ride a kid's tricycle and push a baby doll buggy around the house; I can still picture him on that tricycle with his knees sticking out.

David remembers that when he was about four, our parents bought him a simple model airplane kit consisting of about five pieces. David worked on it for a while and finally got the tail and the fuselage together, but couldn't make further progress no matter how hard he tried. Finally he laid all the pieces down and told Daddy, "I guess we'll just have to read the DESTRUCTIONS." So Daddy read the "destructions" and together they finished the plane. Incidentally, David followed our dad's footsteps, serving in the Army in the Pacific. He joined the Army after high school and served in South Korea, including sixteen months on the DMZ monitoring radio traffic and radar, as the North Koreans frequently violated South Korean airspace.

Dad always worked hard. He initially retired at age 67, but went back to work in his early 70's to help run a big glass installation job in Oklahoma City, before he retired for good.

Change is inevitable. When my dad was in his mid 70's, Mother and Daddy went to the VA hospital to get Daddy's flu shot. Mother called me afterward and said the nurse could pinch a little bit of skin on his biceps when she gave him his shot. His huge biceps were shrinking. Mom said, "Don't mention it to your daddy, it might hurt his feelings." But I think she was the one surprised. My dad knows bodies change with age, but he doesn't always act like he knows it. His grandson still loves to come and arm wrestle him, or they get each other in some hold. Then they laugh and laugh. Grandpa plays with each child on their level—even if that grandchild is now in his twenties. He still enjoys going to a Cardinals baseball game when he visits his St. Louis family.

Baseball, not so much anymore. Battle, that was many years ago, though the physical effects linger. But still, his bride. That's what counts these days.

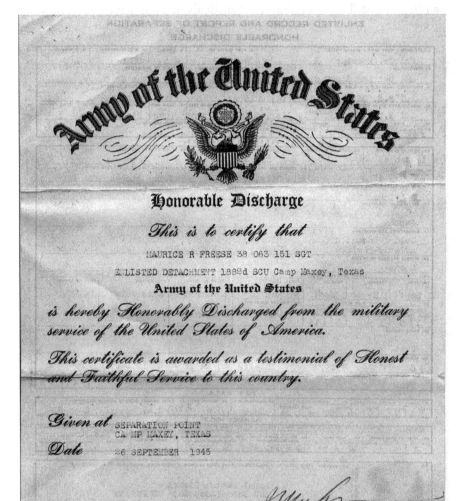

Robert Freese's Honorable Discharge, 26 September 1945-front.

ENLISTED RECORD AND REPORT OF SEPARATION

HONORABLE DISCHARGE

1. LAST NAME - FIRST NAME - MIDDLE INITIAL	2. ARMY SERIAL NO.	3. GRADE	4. ARM OR SERVICE	5. COMPONENT
Freese, Maurice R	38 063 151	Sgt	DEML	AUS

6. ORGANIZATION	7. DATE OF SEPARATION	8. PLACE OF SEPARATION
Enl Det 1882d SCU Cp Maxey, Texas	26 Sep 45	Sep Point Cp Maxey, Texas

9. PERMANENT ADDRESS FOR MAILING PURPOSES	10. DATE OF BIRTH	11. PLACE OF BIRTH
101 S.E. 38th St Okla City, Okla	25 Sep 1916	Oklahoma City, Okla

12. ADDRESS FROM WHICH EMPLOYMENT WILL BE SOUGHT	13. COLOR EYES	14. COLOR HAIR	15. HEIGHT	16. WEIGHT	17. NO. DEPEND.
101 S. E. 38th St Okla City, Okla	Brown	Brown	5' 10"	165	1

18. RACE			19. MARITAL STATUS		20. U.S. CITIZEN		21. CIVILIAN OCCUPATION AND NO.
WHITE	NEGRO	OTHER (specify)	SINGLE	MARRIED	OTHER (specify)	YES X	NO
X				X			Glass Cutter 010

MILITARY HISTORY

22. DATE OF INDUCTION	23. DATE OF ENLISTMENT	24. DATE OF ENTRY INTO ACTIVE SERVICE	25. PLACE OF ENTRY INTO SERVICE
11 Jan 42		11 Jan 42	Ft Sill, Oklahoma

26. SELECTIVE SERVICE DATA	26. REGISTERED	27. LOCAL S.S. BOARD NO.	28. COUNTY AND STATE	29. HOME ADDRESS AT TIME OF ENTRY INTO SERVICE
	YES	NO	2	Okla City, Okla	101 S.E. 38th St Okla City

30. MILITARY OCCUPATIONAL SPECIALTY AND NO.	31. MILITARY QUALIFICATION AND DATE (i.e., infantry, aviation and marksmanship badges, etc.)
Rifleman 745	Combat Infantry Badge

32. BATTLES AND CAMPAIGNS
Papuan

33. DECORATIONS AND CITATIONS
Good Conduct Ribbon
Asiatic-Pacific Theatre Ribbon, 2 Br Stars, Distinguished Unit Badge

34. WOUNDS RECEIVED IN ACTION
None

35.		LATEST IMMUNIZATION DATES		36.	SERVICE OUTSIDE CONTINENTAL U. S. AND RETURN		
SMALLPOX	TYPHOID	TETANUS	OTHER (specify)	DATE OF DEPARTURE	DESTINATION	DATE OF ARRIVAL	
11 Sep44	11 Sep44	18 Nov 43	Yellow Fev 13 Mar 42	22 Apr 42	Australia	14 May 42	

37.	TOTAL LENGTH OF SERVICE				38. HIGHEST GRADE HELD			
CONTINENTAL SERVICE			FOREIGN SERVICE			12 Sep 44	USA	6 Oct 44
YEARS	MONTHS	DAYS	YEARS	MONTHS	DAYS	Sgt		
1	3	1	2	5	14			

39. PRIOR SERVICE
None

40. REASON AND AUTHORITY FOR SEPARATION
Convenience Of Government RR1-1(D em) AR 615-365 15 Dec 1944

41. SERVICE SCHOOLS ATTENDED	42. EDUCATION (Years)	
None	Grammar High School	4 0

PAY DATA

43. LONGEVITY FOR PAY PURPOSES			44. MUSTERING OUT PAY		45. SOLDIER DEPOSITS	46. TRAVEL PAY	47. TOTAL AMOUNT, NAME OF DISBURSING OFFICER
YEARS	MONTHS	DAYS	TOTAL	THIS PAYMENT	None	$15.40	$179.74 W. A. McKenzie, Capt FD
3		27	$300	$100			

INSURANCE NOTICE

IMPORTANT IF PREMIUM IS NOT PAID WHEN DUE OR WITHIN THIRTY-ONE DAYS THEREAFTER, INSURANCE WILL LAPSE. MAKE CHECKS OR MONEY ORDERS PAYABLE TO THE TREASURER OF THE U. S. AND FORWARD TO COLLECTIONS SUBDIVISION, VETERANS ADMINISTRATION, WASHINGTON 25, D. C.

48. KIND OF INSURANCE				49. HOW PAID		50. Effective Date of Allotment Discontinuance	51. Date of Next Premium Due (One month after 50)	52. PREMIUM DUE EACH MONTH	53. INTENTION OF VETERAN TO		
Nat. Serv.	U.S. Govt.	None	Allotment	Direct to V. A.		Continue	Continue Only	Discontinue
X			X			3 0 Sep 45	31 Oct 45	$3.35			X

54.	RIGHT THUMB PRINT	55. REMARKS (This space for completion of above items or entry of other items specified in W. D. Directives)
		Lapel Button Issued
		ASR Score(2 Sep 45) 83 Points
		19 Days Lost Under Article War 107

56. SIGNATURE OF PERSON BEING SEPARATED	57. PERSONNEL OFFICER (Type name, grade and organization - signature)
Maurice R. Freese	JOHN W KENT, CAPT CMP John W Kent

WD AGO FORM 53-55
1 November 1944
This form supersedes all previous editions of WD AGO Forms 53 and 55 for enlisted persons entitled to an Honorable Discharge, which will not be used after...

STATE OF OKLAHOMA, OKLAHOMA COUNTY, SS
I, HELEN NIX, duly elected, qualified and acting County Clerk in and for the county aforesaid, do hereby certify that the within and foregoing is a full, true and complete photostat copy of Discharge filed in the office of the County Clerk on the 27 day of Sept 19 and recorded in book of Discharges 13 at Page 475

HELEN NIX, COUNTY CLERK

Robert Freese's Honorable Discharge, 26 September 1945-back.

149

Bibliography/Notes

Primary Sources

- Many personal and telephonic interviews with Robert and Leona Freese

- Personal letters Robert wrote to Leona throughout WW-II

- E-mails and notes from Robert & Leona's daughter Trish Carnes and son David Freese

Other Sources

INTRODUCTION

1. James Campbell, *The Ghost Mountain Boys*, (New York, NY: Three Rivers Press, 2007), xiii.
2. Dominic J. Caraccilo, "War in Miniature: Bloody Buna," *Veterans of Foreign Wars*, (December 1992): 16.

CHAPTER 1: LIFE IN OKLAHOMA

1. Unattributed, "Gassers Are Forced to Go 11 Innings to Edge Bells, 8-6," *The Oklahoman*, June 14, 1947, 8.
2. Journal Record Staff, "Part IV, Oklahoma City during the 1930s: The only thing we have to," *The Journal Record*, September 2, 2003

3. Oklahoma Historical Society, "Wild Mary Sudik Revisited," Oklahoma Journeys, Week of March 21, 2009, http://www.okhistory.org/okjourneys/sudikrevisited.html.

CHAPTER 2: WORLD WAR II BEGINS

1. 32nd "Red Arrow" Veteran Association, "World War II History of the 32nd Infantry Division," http://www.32nd-division.org/history/ww2/32ww2-1.html#Mobilization

CHAPTER 3: AUSTRALIA

1. Samuel Milner, *The War in the Pacific, Victory in Papua*, (Washington DC: Office of the Chief of Military History, United States Army, 1957, Reprinted 1978), 3.
2. War Department, Historical Division, *Papuan Campaign: The Buna-Sanananda Operation, 16 November 1942-23 January 1943*, (Nashville, TN: The Battery Press, Inc., First Issued 1944), 2.

CHAPTER 4: BATTLING THE ELEMENTS IN NEW GUINEA

1. Samuel Milner, *The War in the Pacific, Victory in Papua*, 56-57.
2. James Campbell, *The Ghost Mountain Boys*, 63-64.
3. Haruko Taya Cook & Theodore F. Cook, *Japan At War: An Oral History*, (New York, NY: The New Press, 1992), 42-43.
4. James Campbell, *The Ghost Mountain Boys*, 143-144.
5. Ibid, 130.
6. Samuel Milner, *The War in the Pacific, Victory in Papua*, 114.

CHAPTER 5: THE BATTLE FOR BUNA BEGINS

1. Harry A. Gailey, *MacArthur Strikes Back, Decision at Buna: New Guinea 1942-1943*, (Novato, CA: Presido Press, Inc., 2000), 140.
2. Samuel Milner, *The War in the Pacific, Victory in Papua*, 170.
3. Ibid, 144.
4. War Department, Historical Division, *Papuan Campaign: The Buna-Sanananda Operation, 16 November 1942-23 January 1943*, 10-11.
5. Samuel Milner, *The War in the Pacific, Victory in Papua*, 176.
6. James Campbell, *The Ghost Mountain Boys*, 152, 179.
7. Samuel Milner, *The War in the Pacific, Victory in Papua*, 177-178.
8. Ibid, 238-240.

CHAPTER 6: DRIVING THE ENEMY OUT OF BUNA

1. Max Hastings, *Retribution: The Battle for Japan, 1944-45*, (New York, NY: Vintage Books, 2007), 26, 49.
2. James Campbell, *The Ghost Mountain Boys*, 275.
3. J. Kahn, Jr., *G.I. Jungle*, (New York, NY: Simon and Schuster, 1943), 121-122.

CHAPTER 8: AMPHIBIOUS ASSAULTS

1. Samuel Milner, *The War in the Pacific, Victory in Papua*, 110.

CHAPTER 10: GOING HOME...AND A BRIDE

1. Max Hastings, *Retribution: The Battle for Japan, 1944-45*, 8.

EPILOGUE

1. Note: The women on the DPCC softball team were Pat Avery, Sherry Bell, Trish Carnes, Doll Comeaux, Jeri Comeaux, Bobbi Cummings, Linda Cummings, Betty Cussin , Claire Elman , Janet Elwood, Denise Followwill, Luann Followwill, Linda Gayski, Joy Hendricks, Doris Jones, Sondra Newcomb, Patty Pryor, Judy Rayburn, Jolene Short, Mavis Smith, Susan Stone, Linda Turner, Lil White, Penny White, and Mary Jo Williams.

Graphics

All photographs, documents, and other graphics are from Robert and Leona's personal collection, except as noted below:

Chapter Two M1 rifle image and Chapter Five M1903 image: Courtesy of tri. army.mil. Tri.army.mil Public Domain notice: *This image is a work of a US Army soldier or employee, made during the course of the person's official duties. As a work of the US federal government, the image is in the public domain.*

Chapter Three maps of Australia and New Guinea: Courtesy of the CIA World Factbook. Public Domain notice: *Unless a copyright is indicated, information on the Central Intelligence Agency Web site is in the public domain and may be reproduced, published or otherwise used without the Central Intelligence Agency's permission. We request only that the Central Intelligence Agency be cited as the source of the information and that any photo credits or bylines be similarly credited to the photographer or author or Central Intelligence Agency, as appropriate.*

Chapter Four T-6 and C-47 photos, Chapter Six P-38 photo: Courtesy of AF.mil. Air Force Public Domain notice: *AF.mil is provided as a public service by the Office of the Secretary of Air Force (Public Affairs). Information presented on AF.mil is considered public information and may be distributed or copied. Use of appropriate byline/photo/image credits is requested.*

Chapter Five Battle Map of the Cape Endaiadere area was made by James Bement.

Printed in the United States
by Baker & Taylor Publisher Services